Spectacular Sisters

Amazing stories of sisters from around the world

Spectacular Sisters

Amazing stories of sisters *From* around the world

Aura Lewis

Quill Tree Books

Quill Tree Books is an imprint of HarperCollins Publishers.
Spectacular Sisters
Text copyright © 2021 by Aura Lewis
Illustrations copyright © 2021 by Aura Lewis
All rights reserved. Printed in Italy.

Library of Congress Cataloging-in-Publication Data

Names: Lewis, Aura, author, illustrator.
Title: Spectacular sisters / [written and illustrated by] Aura Lewis.
Description: First edition. | New York, NY : Quill Tree Books, an imprint of HarperCollins,
    [2021] | Audience: Ages 8-12. | Audience: Grades 4-6. | Summary: "This spectacular,
    diverse biography collection celebrates famous and not-so-famous sisters throughout
    history"-- Provided by publisher.
Identifiers: LCCN 2020032830 | ISBN 978-0-06-294765-9 (hardcover)
Subjects: LCSH: Sisters--Juvenile literature. | Sisters--Case studies.
Classification: LCC HQ759.96 .L48 2021 | DDC 306.875092/2 [B]--dc23
LC record available at https://lccn.loc.gov/2020032830

Typography by Molly Fehr
21 22 23 24 25   RTLO   10 9 8 7 6 5 4 3 2 1
❖

First Edition

**To Deena and Darya,
with love**

Maxine   Patty   LaVerne

Mag   Louisa

Emily   Elizabeth

Anna   Elena

Catherine   Harriet

Claribel   Etta

Ida   Louisa

Emily   Charlotte   Anne

Pauline
(Dear Abby)

Esther
(Ann Landers)

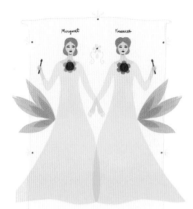

Margaret   Francesca

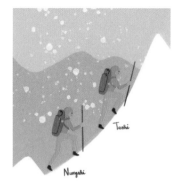

Tashi

Nungshi

Linda   Joananna

Tatyana   Hannah

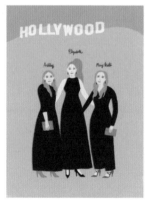

Pippa   Kate

Rita   Laura

Malia   Sasha

HOLLYWOOD

Ashley   Elizabeth   Mary-Kate

Patria   Maria Theresa   Minerva

Dedé

Margaret   Roumania

Stefania Helena

Barbara Diana

Ai-ling

Mei-ling

Qing-ling

Edythe Coretta

Tree

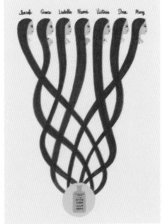

Jacob Grace Isabella Naomi Victoria Dina Mary

Mary Elizabeth

Vanessa Virginia

Venus

Serena

Contents

Introduction

*"She is your partner in crime, your midnight companion,
someone who knows when you are smiling even in the dark."*
—Barbara Alpert

*"If your sister is in a tearing hurry to go out and cannot
catch your eye, she's wearing your best sweater."*
—Pam Brown

I am a sister times four.

I am super lucky to have two sisters AND two brothers. I couldn't imagine what it would be like to live without them.

I'm also surrounded by sisters.

I have three daughters, who remind me on a daily basis what it's like to be a sister and to grow up with one (shared bedrooms, hand-me-down clothing, taking turns with toys, and couch snuggling).

Did you know that having a sister is actually good for you? It makes you happier and healthier! Lots of girls and women say that talking with their sister comforts them through the ups and downs of life. Sisters help each other deal with stress and be more emotionally balanced. They are there no matter what—through the good and the bad.

But having a sister can also be, well, complex. Sometimes things can get rocky, frustrating, or downright annoying—like when your sister wears your shirt and gets all the compliments! It can be hard to be a sister, especially when she's being critical or competitive.

And yet, a sister can be your confidante, your biggest cheerleader, and of course your fashion stylist! You can count on her to give you honest opinions and to help you survive family events. A sister is a lifelong best friend.

Bottom line: sisters are the best.

This book celebrates all kinds of sisters. Some lived a long time ago; some are contemporary. Sometimes one of the sisters is more famous than the other, and then it's interesting to find out about the lesser-known one. Some of the sisters worked together, or had similar professions, while others chose to lead very different lives. Some sisters are heroic and inspirational, while others have more complicated backgrounds. But all the sisters have interesting stories. And all made their marks on the world in their own ways.

Louisa May & Abigail May Alcott

American novelist and artist

Louisa May (1832–1888)
Abigail May (1840–1879)

You have probably heard of the novel *Little Women*, about the four March sisters. This novel has enchanted millions of readers since it was published in 1868 and was adapted multiple times to the big screen.

Yet not many know much about the author, Louisa. *Little Women* was inspired by her own life growing up with three sisters, of which she was the second born. Louisa had a close relationship with all three but especially with the youngest, Abigail, always referred to as May, with whom she shared an artistic sensibility.

The sisters grew up in Orchard House, in Concord, Massachusetts. Their parents were teachers and made only a small income. Louisa helped out by taking on teaching, needlework, and even domestic service, like washing laundry. During the Civil War, she worked as a military nurse. But her heart was not in any of it. Her passion was always for writing, and she wrote whenever she could. She sent lengthy letters to her sisters about her wartime experiences.

Eventually, these letters became her first book, *Hospital Sketches*. She also wrote novellas and poems, as well as spy stories, under the name of A. M. Barnard. When she was asked to write a novel for girls, Louisa was stumped. Not sure how to proceed, she wrote about what she knew best: her own life. And lo and behold, *Little Women* became an instant success. The

"Oh my girls, however long you may live, I never can wish you a greater happiness than this!"

book resonated with young women because it portrayed them as taking active roles in their own lives. By doing so, it broke all stereotypes. Louisa became famous overnight!

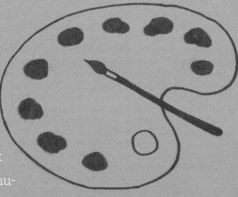

In addition to being an accomplished author, Louisa was an abolitionist and an early feminist. In 1879, Massachusetts granted women the right to vote in local elections on issues involving education and children. Louisa registered right away and became the first woman to do so in Concord! She went door to door and encouraged women to vote.

Louisa's fame brought her wealth, which she did not have growing up. She even made enough money to support May, who had a dream of studying painting in Europe. The sisters always longed to leave the little town of Concord, and in 1870, Louisa joined May on a grand European tour. May eventually married and stayed to live with her husband in Paris.

Though May and Louisa had a close relationship, Louisa often felt jealous of May's family life; Louisa herself never married. May was also the youngest and prettiest of the sisters, and she was considered "the queen" by their father. As you can imagine, this stirred Louisa's envy as well.

In 1879, May wrote about her experiences in the book *Studying Art Abroad: And How to Do It Cheaply*. She had a daughter whom she named Louisa (Lulu) after her older sister. Sadly, May died shortly after childbirth. Her last wish was that Louisa raise Lulu, as Ernest, her husband, traveled widely for work. Accordingly, Lulu went to live with her devoted aunt Louisa. And so, until Louisa's own death in 1888, the two lived together, with Louisa finally having a little family of her own.

LaVerne, Maxene & Patty Andrews

Popular American singing group in the 1930s and 1940s

LaVerne (1911–1967), Maxene (1916–1995),
Patty (1918–2013)

The Andrews Sisters—LaVerne, Maxene, and Patty—loved music from a young age. They would stand together around their family piano in Minneapolis, Minnesota, and sing songs from their favorite bands. Their voices complemented each other: LaVerne sang contralto, Maxene was a mezzo-soprano, and Patty sang soprano. In 1931, during spring break from school, they entered and won a talent contest together and were invited to tour around the Midwest with a local band. At first, their father was reluctant to let the sisters leave school at such a young age (Patty was just a young teenager at the time), but their mother convinced him, and off they went.

After singing professionally for six years, in 1937, LaVerne, Maxene, and Patty finally got their first big break: they recorded the song "Bei Mir Bist Du Schoen" (which translates to "you are beautiful in my eyes"). The song was originally written for the Yiddish theater, but they sang an English version. All their songs were written by others. The song sold 350,000 copies and immediately launched them as celebrities! From then on, their fame just grew. The three sisters quickly became one of America's most popular singing groups and one of the best-selling women's vocal groups of all time. They were so successful that they sold almost one hundred million records! They performed on Broadway, on radio (they hosted their own hit radio show, *The Andrews Sisters Show*), and in several Hollywood films. Even Elvis Presley, the famous rock 'n' roll star, was a huge fan.

In the 1940s, at the height of their success, World War II was underway. The sisters took on patriotic duties and were extremely active in the war effort. They volunteered to sing to wounded soldiers and performed for thousands of military personnel overseas. They also recorded "Victory Discs" for the soldiers. "Victory Discs" were records produced especially for US military personnel during the war in order to boost their morale. The sisters sang famous songs like "Boogie Woogie Bugle Boy." Their music was always upbeat and cheerful, which provided an escape for the soldiers from the harsh reality of the war. For their efforts during this time, the sisters were nicknamed "America's Wartime Sweethearts."

In the 1950s, their luck waned and things got a little messy. The sisters' group broke up; Patty pursued a solo career, while LaVerne and Maxene continued to sing together. In 1956, they reunited, but they never had the same success as before. Nevertheless, they will always be remembered as the stars they were. People loved the Andrews Sisters not only for their bold vocal harmonies and musical variety but also for their charming personalities and lighthearted humor.

The Azmi Sisters

Field hockey players and advocates for girls' rights and religious freedom

Asiyah (born 1993), Nuha (born 1995), Husnah (born 1997),
Sajidah (born 2000), Haleemah (born 2001),
Mubeenah (born 2004)

*"Our advice to young girls is to challenge every barrier they
face and to not compromise any part of who they are,
because hockey is a sport that's meant for everyone."*
—The Azmi sisters

These athletic sisters are not your typical hockey players. On the field, they are decked out in the usual sports gear—shin pads, helmets, and hockey gloves. And also hijabs.

The six sisters come from a Pakistani Muslim family, and they were born and raised in Toronto, Canada.

Their dad, Shaheen Azmi, who emigrated from Pakistan as a toddler, is a huge ice hockey fan. He and his wife, Fara, enrolled their three sons—the sisters' brothers—in ice hockey classes. Shaheen got his daughters into skating and hockey too. But since he and his wife couldn't afford the expensive ice hockey gear for their daughters, they sent the sisters to play field hockey instead. From a young age, the sisters fell in love with the game and kept playing until they got better and better.

As adults, the sisters have played in the summer league of the Toronto Women's Ball Hockey Association as well as in the Ontario Women's fall hockey league. The audiences who attend their games are often taken aback when the sisters enter wearing hijabs, an uncommon sight on Canadian hockey fields. The spectators have no idea what to expect! But they are pleasantly surprised when they see how well the sisters play. The Azmis embrace this; they want to break stereotypes of what a hockey player looks like, and even what a Canadian looks like. They want to prove that they are as good as everyone else when it comes to playing sports.

The Azmi sisters care deeply about their religion, and make a point of showing that they don't have to compromise their religious beliefs in order to play hockey. This is not always easy. They make time to pray five times a day, between their practice and games. One particularly challenging moment was during the month of Ramadan, in which practicing Muslims fast all day and eat only after sundown. The Toronto Women's Ball Hockey Association accommodated the Azmis and held all the games at nine in the evening, so the sisters could eat and drink after sundown and have energy to play.

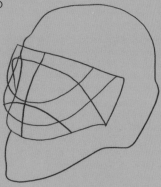

In addition, the sisters believe in women's empowerment. They want to promote sports among Muslim women, and they hope to inspire future generations of girls. The Azmis speak up about these issues and have gotten a lot of Canadian press for being champions of women's rights, religious freedom, and inclusion in sports.

The Azmi sisters' passion for hockey is a great way for the sisters to connect with each other. The game literally brings them closer together—though they are the first to admit they've had many a fight over the game! At home, the six sisters share a bedroom, which is totally covered in hockey trinkets and paraphernalia, like posters and pillows. On the field, even when they're competing with opponents, the sisters feel reassured and comforted to be near each other. Because they're so close, and know each other so well, they're a winning team!

Anna & Elena Balbusso

Italian artists and illustrators

Anna (born 1975)
Elena (born 1975)

Most artists work alone, but not the Balbusso sisters. Anna and Elena, identical twins from Italy, have always done everything together. Since they were three years old, they drew together, and today as adults, they continue to make art together. They work jointly to create all their pieces, and share the credit for each image. They sign their work: A+E=Balbusso.

Anna and Elena both went to art high school, where they studied design, photography, and printmaking. Then they continued to study painting at the Accademia di Brera in Milan. The sisters became experts in drawing, color, and composition as well as design. At first, they presented their work separately to publishing houses and other businesses. But editors and art directors who met with them thought it was too confusing. Not only were the sisters identical, but their work is very similar as well! So the sisters created a single artistic identity, and that's when they began to be successful.

How do they work on a single piece together? The sisters begin by sharing their vision for each piece. They do a lot of research, and they are inspired by art history. Their work is a true collaboration: they come up with the composition together; neither dictates any image. When they actually paint, Anna is the expert in faces, while Elena often works on the textures and patterns. They love making art together, and for them, two is better than one.

"For us it is as natural as drinking a glass of water. We share the successes but also the difficulties and fatigue."

Their work has a painterly style and medieval influences and has been described as "enticingly Renaissance and eerily new wave" by art critics. In recent years, their works have evolved to be more graphic as well, inspired by a futuristic aesthetic.

The sisters live and work for part of the year in New York City and in Milan, Italy, for the rest. They make art and illustrations for big magazines all over the world, and they have illustrated more than forty books for children and adults. Their work has also been exhibited in many museums and is internationally acclaimed. Anna and Elena have won so many awards and illustration medals (more than seventy international awards and counting!) that if there were art olympics, the Balbusso twins would surely break all the records.

Harriet Beecher Stowe & Catharine Esther Beecher

Educators, writers, and abolitionists

Catharine (1800–1878)
Harriet (1811–1896)

Harriet and Catharine were two of thirteen children of Lyman Beecher, a prominent Evangelical priest. From a young age, they saw their father's dedication to public service and looked up to him.

When Harriet was only seven years old, she won her school's essay contest. She was very proud, and more so, she was delighted that she made her father proud too. From that moment on, Harriet's quill rarely left her hand. It also didn't hurt that she had an older sister as a role model; Catharine loved to write as well.

Like their father, each sister in her own way devoted her life to a public cause. Catharine promoted equal education for women and founded several schools and colleges for women (Harriet attended one of them: the Hartford Female Seminary in Connecticut). She also wrote several books, the most famous of which is *A Treatise on Domestic Economy* from 1841. In the book, Catharine discusses work related to taking care of the home and argues that women can influence American society by being homemakers. According to historian Kathryn Sklar, Catharine became known as an expert on everything to do with the American home and its well-being.

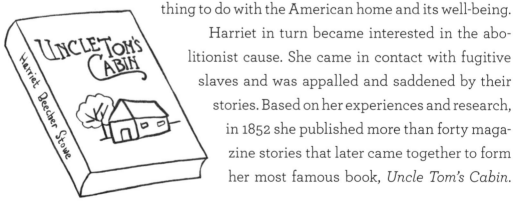

Harriet in turn became interested in the abolitionist cause. She came in contact with fugitive slaves and was appalled and saddened by their stories. Based on her experiences and research, in 1852 she published more than forty magazine stories that later came together to form her most famous book, *Uncle Tom's Cabin*.

The book, which promotes antislavery ideas, immediately became a sensation in the North, but it was widely criticized in the slave-owning South. Although Harriet was an advocate for abolition, she also created characters in her writing that reflected negatively on Black childhood experiences. In many ways, the book shaped Americans' views of slavery, and some say even partly led to the American Civil War in 1861. Harriet met with President Lincoln, who reportedly greeted her by saying, "So you are the little woman who wrote the book that started this great war." Harriet published more than thirty books.

Harriet and Catharine were always close, and in 1869, they wrote an advice book together called *The American Woman's Home*, which was a continuation of Catharine's *Treatise*. In the book, they speak about the important role of women at home and with their families. It continues both sisters' lifelong beliefs and their support of women's strengths and abilities.

Emily & Elizabeth Blackwell

American physicians and pioneers
in women's medicine

Elizabeth (1821–1910)
Emily (1826–1910)

Emily

Elizabeth

Elizabeth's close friend was dying. She told Elizabeth that if her physician had been a woman, she would have suffered less. At that time, many people thought that women should not and could not be good scientists and doctors. But her friend's words burned in Elizabeth, and she decided she had to become a doctor. To people who thought she wouldn't make it, Elizabeth simply said, "As to the opinion of people, I don't care one straw personally." She was determined, and she went after her dream.

Elizabeth and her younger sister Emily were born in England, and in 1832 moved with their large family to the United States when they were eleven and six, respectively. They grew up in a home that was deeply spiritual and devoted to social reform, such as abolition (the movement to end slavery). Elizabeth grew up to believe that health was closely related to morality, and that women, with their superior moral sense, are very well suited for the medical field. By practicing medicine, they can contribute to making society better.

However, in reality, becoming a doctor was almost impossible for women. Elizabeth was rejected again and again from every school she applied to, simply because of her gender. When she was finally admitted to a school in rural New York, it was as a practical joke! And as a student, Elizabeth faced lots of discrimination, both from her peers and from her teachers too. For example, she was made to sit separately and wasn't permitted in certain labs. But Elizabeth did not give up! In 1849, she not only graduated first in her class, but she also became the first woman to receive a medical degree in the United States. Elizabeth's younger sister Emily was so inspired by

Elizabeth's courage and her achievement that she decided to become a physician herself. In 1854, she became the third woman to get a medical degree in the United States.

But things were not easy for the Blackwell sisters. Elizabeth could not find a hospital that would employ her, and she had to leave for France. Emily, too, had to travel to Europe to complete her education as a surgeon, as universities in the United States closed their doors to her. The sisters decided to take matters into their own hands. In 1857, Elizabeth, Emily, and their colleague Dr. Marie Zakrzewska established the New York Infirmary for Indigent Women and Children, where women could get a high-quality medical education and where women doctors could work. By 1874, the infirmary served more than seven thousand patients every year! It was the first hospital run by women and the first dedicated to serving women and children in the United States. The Blackwell sisters paved the way for women physicians in America, and they went down in history as pioneers in promoting the education of women in medicine and health.

The Bouvier Sisters
Jacqueline Kennedy Onassis
& Lee Radziwill

American First Lady and former Polish princess

Jacqueline "Jackie" (1929–1994)
Caroline Lee (1933–2019)

Jacqueline "Jackie" Kennedy Onassis and Lee Radziwill were both grand and glamorous women and style icons of the twentieth century. The sisters were born to the wealthy and stylish "Black Jack" and Janet Bouvier, who brought them up to sparkle. Jackie was considered beautiful, bright, and charismatic, but she was also somewhat mischievous. Her teacher said she was "a darling child, the prettiest little girl, very clever, very artistic, and full of the devil." Lee was also pretty, clever, and adventurous. However, she was always somewhat in her older sister's shadow, who dazzled everyone she came in contact with. This was something that persisted through the rest of their lives.

When they grew up, both sisters worked for a while in the journalism world. Jackie became a journalistic photographer for the *Washington Times-Herald*, where she interviewed and met many politicians and dignitaries. Among them was John F. Kennedy (JFK), who was a congressman for Massachusetts at the time. They fell in love and married in 1953. Jackie helped him campaign for the presidency, and in 1960, JFK was elected thirty-fifth president of the United States. The whole family moved to the White House, and Jackie, who was only thirty-one, became First Lady at his inauguration in 1961. She was a trendsetter, and people loved her for bringing youthful style and artistic spirit to the White House.

In the meantime, Lee was an assistant to fashion editor and icon Diana Vreeland at *Harper's Bazaar*. In 1959, she married Polish prince Stanislas Radziwill, making her a princess. In her lifetime, she attempted a career in acting and starred on Broadway  as well as on TV. Unfortunately, she was poorly received. Later, she tried her luck as an interior decorator, but she was not successful at that either. She was friends with many celebrities and even toured with the band the Rolling Stones alongside her friend, author Truman Capote.

Jackie and Lee were close confidantes for much of their lives, and they shared a love for beauty, art, design, and fashion. They spent many holidays together, and in 1962 they vacationed in Italy, India, and Pakistan for a month. In 1963, John F. Kennedy was tragically assassinated, leaving behind a shocked and grieving Jackie and her two children. Lee hurried from London to help her sister in the crisis. One small example of her care was leaving a note on Jackie's pillow telling her how much she admired her strength. All this being said, Jackie and Lee had a complex relationship too, which included jealousy and rivalry, to the point that Jackie did not leave anything for Lee in her will.

Charlotte, Emily & Anne Brontë

English poets and novelists

Charlotte (1816–1855), Emily (1818–1848),
Anne (1820–1849)

Angria and Gondal: these were the magical names of the imaginary worlds that sisters Charlotte, Emily, and Anne, along with their younger brother, Branwell, spent hours inventing. They wrote their stories, which were often quite dramatic, in tiny matchbox-sized books. The siblings hand-made them, complete with detailed maps, tiny illustrations, and even hand-lettered advertisements! The words in the books were so miniscule that the grown-ups couldn't read them.

The Brontë sisters' lives were not so magical though. When they were very young, their mother and two older sisters died of different illnesses. Their family was poor, so Charlotte, Emily, and Anne had to get jobs to make ends meet. They tried working as teachers and governesses, but all three were desperately unhappy. Charlotte was easily irritable and felt that she worked with "fat-headed oafs." Anne was subdued and didn't often voice her opinions, though she was also displeased. Emily at one time told her students that she preferred the school dog to them. (Emily loved animals more than most things and had a variety of pets, including several dogs and a hawk named Nero.)

What the Brontë sisters did have, however, was access to their father's library. They grew up with a deep love of books, and from the moment they made their matchbox books as girls, the sisters wanted to become bookmakers and writers.

But in the nineteenthth century, it was not considered appropriate for women to be authors. In the words of Robert Southey, England's poet laureate at the time, "literature cannot be the business of a woman's life, and it ought not to be."

The three sisters would not be stopped. They found a solution: they took on male pseudonyms and published a joint book of poems under the names of Currer (Charlotte), Ellis (Emily), and Acton (Anne) Bell. Their book sold only two copies though, so they gave up poetry and turned to prose. In 1947, Charlotte published *Jane Eyre*, which quickly became a massive hit. That same year, Emily published *Wuthering Heights*, and Anne published *Agnes Grey*. A year later, in 1848, they finally revealed their true identities to everyone's astonishment and disbelief. After the initial shock, the sisters were celebrated in London for who they were.

The Brontë sisters' novels are admired for giving a voice to ordinary women who make their own way. They offer readers a glimpse into the lives of women from that time. Though the sisters did not publish much, their novels became huge classics of English literature, and they are still read worldwide today.

Claribel & Etta Cone

American art collectors who introduced
important painters to the United States

Claribel (1864–1929)
Etta (1870–1949)

Have you ever heard of the painters Matisse, Cézanne, or Picasso? Well, largely thanks to Claribel and Etta Cone, these and more avant-garde artists came to be known and appreciated in the United States back in the early twentieth century, when modern art was still considered strange at best. The sisters, originally from Baltimore, Maryland, were born to a newly wealthy German-Jewish family, two out of thirteen children. The sisters were always very close, and they lived in adjoining apartments for fifty years. And yet, they had very different personalities: Claribel, who was known as flamboyant, highly independent, and assertive, became a physician and a pathologist against the wishes of her parents. (At the time there were only a handful of women physicians worldwide!) Throughout her career, she conducted research and worked as a professor at a female college. She was also an advocate for women's suffrage and health-care rights. Etta, who was quieter and more reflective, was an accomplished pianist and had an interest in art.

Neither sister was married, and both had money to spare, so starting in 1901 they began traveling annually to Europe, following Etta's love for anything French. The sisters visited churches, museums, and gardens and bought paintings they

loved. It didn't take long for them to become
art collectors. Claribel said she always
loved to collect beautiful things: "Ever
since I was a small girl and picked up
all the shells I could find, reveling in
their color and in their forms." As in
their personalities, Claribel's taste in
art was bolder than Etta's. In Europe,
they became friends with the greatest
European artists and socialites of the time,
and they spent hours in the Parisian salons.

They were close friends with literary illuminati Gertrude Stein, who wrote
about them in her essay "Two Women." The Cone sisters were also depicted
in drawings by their artist friends, Henri Matisse and Pablo Picasso.

Over their lifetime, the sisters collected more than three thousand works
of art, including paintings, objects, jewelry, and furniture from all over the
world. The sisters loved to shop so much that when they would purchase
tickets to the opera during their travels, they would buy three seats: two for
them, and one for their shopping bags! They decorated their small apartments with their massive collections. At the end of their lives, they donated
their vast collection to the Baltimore Museum of Art, where you can see it
today. Their collection is considered one of the most important of its kind in
the world.

Ida & Louise Cook

English novelist and opera lovers
who saved Jews during World War II

Louise (1901–1999)
Ida (1904–1986)

Ida   Louise

These brave and bold sisters saved dozens of people's lives, but they weren't always so daring. Ida and Louise lived with their parents in South London, and both worked as civil service secretaries. One day, after hearing Puccini, the great Italian composer from the late nineteenth century, they developed a deep love of opera. The sisters became huge fans, and they wanted to see the opera stars of the day perform onstage across Europe. The only problem was, they lacked the funds to travel. So Ida began writing romance novels under the pseudonym Mary Burchell in order to make some extra money. Eventually she became a best-selling author! After saving up, the sisters were able to realize their dream. Between 1934 and 1939, they traveled repeatedly to Germany and Austria in order to visit different opera houses and see the stars. During this time, the Nazi political party held power in Germany. Starting in 1933, they established laws that stripped the rights from Jewish people, Romanis, people of color, disabled people, people with different sexual orientations, and other minorities. It was no longer safe for these groups to live there.

On one of their trips, the Cook sisters were alerted by a friend to the terrible plight of the Jews under the Nazi regime. Louise and Ida were horrified and decided they had to help.

The sisters continued to visit opera houses and mingle with high-ranking German officials, such as Joseph Goebbels (the Nazi minister of propaganda) and Heinrich Himmler (one of the most powerful Nazi architects of the Holocaust). But in secret, they were actually rescuing Jews by smuggling them into England. In total, the sisters heroically saved twenty-nine people from the impending Holocaust. The sis-

ters also repeatedly smuggled belongings of the refugees by wearing fur coats and expensive jewelry while crossing the borders. These were serious crimes, and they were risking their lives by doing so. In 1965, the sisters were honored as "Righteous Among the Nations" by the State of Israel for saving so many lives.

The sisters' story is shrouded with mystery to this day. It seems like there's a big piece missing: How did Ida and Louise, who did not make large salaries as secretaries, fund their multiple trips to Germany, their stays in luxury hotels, as well as the expensive opera tickets? The money they made could not have possibly paid for their lavish trips, even with Ida's extra income as an author. Also, how did their repeated travels not arouse suspicion among the Germans? Some think they received help from people in Germany. But more than that, there is a suspicion that they may have actually worked as spies for the British government! The sisters were in a position to gather a lot of intelligence during their trips. The government may have supported their travels as well as provided funding and guarantees to help the Jewish refugees cross the borders into England. Although there are CIA files about the sisters, at this point, all these theories are mere speculations.

Mary & Carrie Dann

Shoshone women who fought
for their ancestral land

Mary (1923–2005)
Carrie (born 1932)

Mary and Carrie Dann were Western Shoshone sisters, elders, and spiritual leaders. They were born in Nevada in 1923 and 1932, respectively, and grew up raising cattle and horses on their tribal lands.

Their story starts a long time ago with their elders. Back in 1868, the Western Shoshone signed the Treaty of Ruby Valley with the US government. This treaty allowed the government to travel through their lands, build a railroad, and even mine for gold (Western Shoshone land was composed of two-thirds of Nevada as well as small parts of California, Idaho, and Utah). However, over time, the government broke the treaty, seizing portions of their territory until it claimed almost 90 percent of the Western Shoshone's ancestral land. To make things worse, the government began conducting nuclear tests in the region and demanded that Shoshone people pay grazing fees for using their own land. In 1974, they even arrested the Dann sisters for trespassing on government property.

Mary and Carrie were beyond furious. They wanted the right to live and farm freely on their lands, just as their people had done for generations. They saw the land as sacred, and Earth as their mother. Taking land was akin to taking a life. It was a spiritual death.

The sisters decided to challenge the United States government, with not only a legal battle in court, but also in their daily lives: they continued to farm their lands as usual, even though it was considered illegal by the government. Finally, in 1979, the court ruled that the government had indeed broken the treaty. However, instead of upholding the treaty and returning the land to the Shoshone people, the court awarded the Western Shoshone twenty-six million dollars. Were the tribal members pleased? Not one bit! They voted to decline the money. After the ruling, the government continued to sue the Western Shoshone for trespassing, and when they didn't comply, it seized all their livestock—more than four hundred horses. Carrie said, "I was Indigenous and in one single evening I was indigent. If you think the Indian wars are over, then think again."

The Danns continued to protest and formed the Western Shoshone Defense Project, which advocated in court for the tribal rights to their land. Their case reached the 1985 Supreme Court in *US v. Dann*, but the court upheld its previous decision to award money instead of returning land. Again, the sisters did not give up.

In 1993, Mary and Carrie received the Right Livelihood Award, an international prize to "honor and support courageous people and organizations offering visionary and exemplary solutions to the root causes of global problems." The sisters won for "exemplary courage and perseverance in asserting the rights of Indigenous people to their land." Mary died in an accident in 2005, but Carrie continues the fight for Western Shoshone land as well as for the rights of Indigenous people throughout the world, now with the support of people in Congress and the United Nations.

Annie Elizabeth & Sarah Louise Delany

American educators and civil rights pioneers

Sarah Louise "Sadie" (1889–1999)
Annie Elizabeth "Bessie" (1891–1995)

"Life is short, and it's up to you to make it sweet."
—Sadie Delany

Sisters Sadie and Bessie lived a VERY long life together: Bessie lived to be 104, and Sadie lived to be 109! Throughout the century of their lives, they were both involved in advocating for civil rights. They each did this in their own style, as they had almost opposite personalities. Sadie was more reserved, calm, and sweet-natured. She protested against discrimination in her quiet way, like sitting in the white section in a store without making a fuss. Bessie, on the other hand, was more confrontational, vivacious, and outgoing, and after a near encounter with the Ku Klux Klan, she was outspoken about advocating for equality.

Sadie and Bessie were born in the segregated South to Henry Beard Delaney, a former enslaved man and a bishop in the Episcopal Church. Their mother was Nanny James Logan, an educator who was light-skinned and could pass as white but was considered "colored" because her mother was a quarter Black. From an early age, the sisters encountered racism; everything was segregated, from the water fountains at the park to the drugstores where they couldn't get service. But Sadie and Bessie did not let these be obstacles to their dreams of success. They worked as teachers and saved money so they could attend college. Their mother then informed them that they must choose between having a family

and a career (at the time, it was hard for women to have full-time careers if they had a family). Sadie and Bessie both chose to focus on their careers and never married.

In 1916, Sadie moved to Harlem in New York City, and Bessie joined her in 1917. It was the beginning of the Harlem Renaissance, and new forms of jazz, literature, and art were flourishing. The sisters enjoyed what the city had to offer, but they stayed devoted to their work. Sadie became the first Black domestic science teacher in a public New York City high school. She got her job without disclosing her heritage, and when the school found out, it was too late to fire her. Bessie became a well-known dentist in Harlem (she was the second Black woman to be licensed as a dentist in New York State). Both were beloved in their community.

Later in life, the sisters moved together to Mount Vernon, a white suburb in New York State. By doing so, they were part of a quiet revolutionary movement to integrate white communities. The sisters became famous only after turning one hundred, when Amy Hill Hearth, a journalist for the *New York Times*, wrote an article about them. The article eventually was expanded into a best-selling book, *Having Our Say: The Delany Sisters' First 100 Years*. Their story was so well received that it was made into a Broadway play in 1995 and into a CBS film in 1999.

Amelia & Muriel Earhart

American aviator and educator

Amelia (1897–1937)
Grace Muriel (1899–1998)

Growing up in Kansas, Amelia and Grace Muriel (who just went by Muriel) did everything together. Amelia, nicknamed "Meeley," and Muriel, called "Pidge," rode horses, shared a love of animals, and played for hours in make-believe games, like an imaginative journey on an elephant's

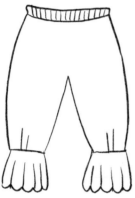

back to the jungle. The sisters, especially Amelia, enjoyed activities that were considered "tomboy-ish," such as tree climbing, sledding, and hunting rats. Unlike most girls at the time, who wore dresses and skirts while playing, Amelia and Muriel wore "bloomers," an early form of pants. Their aunt Margaret was a feminist, and she encouraged her nieces to play in more comfortable clothes.

When Amelia and Muriel grew up, they chose different career paths but remained close. Amelia fell in love with airplanes and decided she must learn to fly, even though very few women did so at the time. But Amelia did not let this stop her; like her aunt, she was a feminist and believed women could do anything men could. In 1921, after saving up enough money, Amelia was able to buy her own airplane, which she painted bright yellow. Before long, she became a record-breaking and world-famous celebrity pilot. She kept pushing her limits, and in 1932, Amelia became the first woman to fly solo across the Atlantic Ocean! She received the United States Distinguished Flying Cross for her amazing achievement. First Lady Eleanor Roosevelt flew with her once and 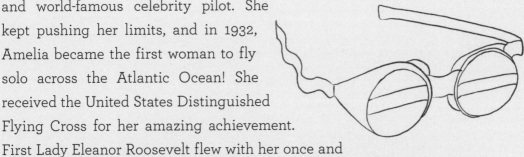 said about her, "She helped the cause of women by giving them a feeling that there was nothing they could not do."

In 1937, while trying to fly around the globe, Amelia tragically and mysteriously disappeared over the Pacific Ocean. To this day, there is a continued fascination in popular culture and media with her life and disappearance. Amelia is remembered as a feminist icon and an inspiration for girls and women to follow their dreams.

Muriel had quite a different life than Amelia. She became an educator and taught English in several high schools in Massachusetts. However, like her older sister, she was also a very active member in her community and was engaged in local politics. For example, she served on the school committee, was a member of the Daughters of the American Revolution, and was active in the League of Women Voters. For these, Muriel was awarded the "Citizen of the Year" in 1979 by the Medford Chamber of Commerce, the town where she resided. Muriel also loved to write, and she published articles in professional magazines, as well as composing poetry. Muriel always sorely missed her dear sister, Amelia, and in 1963 she wrote her biography, *Courage Is the Price*.

Mary & Emily Edmonson

Legends in the fight against slavery

Mary (1832–1853)
Emily (1835–1895)

In 2010, a ten-foot-tall bronze sculpture was erected in Alexandria, Virginia. The sculpture, by artist Erik Blome, is of two sisters, Mary and Emily Edmonson. Who were they?

Mary and Emily Edmonson were born in Maryland in the 1830s to Amelia, who was enslaved, and to Paul, who was freed by his owner. Though their father was free, Maryland law stated that children receive the status of their mother, and so the sisters were enslaved from birth. However, the whole family were considered "Black aristocracy," as they worked as house slaves in family homes and hotels (as opposed to most who worked as field slaves and had a lower status).

When the sisters were young teenagers, they went to work in Washington, DC. There, they were part of a group who planned an escape to freedom. The group, which had seventy-seven people, walked out one night to a small ship, named *Pearl*, which was subsidized by free Black men and white abolitionists. The ship was headed to Philadelphia, a free city in the north. It was the biggest escape attempt by enslaved people in the history of the United States, and it was extremely dangerous, but the enslaved were hopeful and determined.

Unfortunately, the escape attempt failed. Most of the enslaved people aboard were captured and sold to the Deep South, including Mary and Emily. The price for the sisters was set at $1,200—a fortune

at the time—because they were young, pretty, and light-skinned. Paul, the sisters' father, was intent on buying their freedom. With the help of Brooklyn-based pastor Henry Ward Beecher (brother of Harriet and Catharine Beecher, see page 20), Paul was able to raise enough money to free the two sisters. Mary and Emily were emancipated in 1848, and they attended school in New York. The sisters quickly became poster girls for the abolitionist cause. They began to tour the north with Beecher, telling their story of being enslaved, escape, and freedom in order to raise awareness to the anti slavery movement. They had beautiful voices and often sang to the crowds.

In 1853, the sisters attended Oberlin College in Ohio, which had accepted Black students since its founding in 1830.

Sadly, Mary died young of tuberculosis and wasn't able to complete her studies. Emily married and had four children, and she maintained a lifelong friendship with abolitionist leader Frederick Douglass.

Today, you can visit the statue in the sisters' honor in Alexandria. It is placed near the former facility that sold the seventy-seven enslaved people slaves back in 1848. Appropriately, the city named the plaza after the sisters: Edmonson Plaza.

Magda, Zsa Zsa & Eva Gabor

Hungarian-American actresses and socialites

Magda (1915–1997), Zsa Zsa (1917–2016),
Eva (1919–1995)

Magda, Zsa Zsa (born Sari), and Eva were born to an upper-middle-class Jewish family in Budapest, Hungary. Their glamorous mother, Jolie, loved fashion and dressed her daughters—and herself—in matching dresses. The ambitious Jolie was an aspiring actress and planned to groom her daughters to become world-famous stars. She sent Magda, Zsa Zsa, and Eva to dancing, singing, and acting classes. She also took them to the theater on a weekly basis so that they would "get stardust in their eyes." In 1936, her dreams became a reality when Zsa Zsa won the title of Miss Hungary.

In those days, Europe became a harsh place for Jews (see more about this on page 36). So a few years later, the Gabors left Budapest to escape World War II and moved to Hollywood to pursue their dreams of cinematic fame. The three sisters all became actresses and led glamorous and glittery lives, like their mother intended for them. The three divas were "famous for being famous," and were described as the human version of "cotton candy."

Zsa Zsa, the most well-known of the three, made appearances in more than sixty films for the big screen and television, both in the United States and abroad. Magda and Eva also acted in films as well as performed on Broadway. Magda told the *New Yorker* in the 1960s, "I'm a very serious person. I couldn't have built up this idiotic image of myself all these years if I hadn't been serious."

Beyond being known for their acting and their lavish lifestyles, the sisters

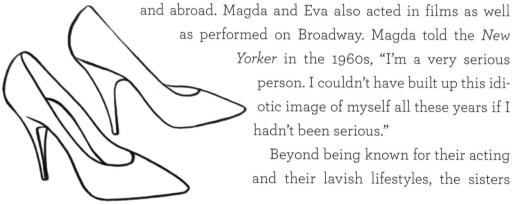

had another claim to fame: they were all married multiple times to different millionaires or famous men. Magda was married six times, Eva five times, and Zsa Zsa a whopping nine times! They even shared a husband: George Sanders, a British actor, was first married to Zsa Zsa and later to Magda. On this topic Zsa Zsa said, "A girl must marry for love and keep on marrying until she finds it." Though the sisters tied the knot so many times, only Zsa Zsa had a child: Francesca Hilton, born in 1947, to her then husband Conrad Hilton.

The sisters were at once admired for their beauty and luxury but also ridiculed and parodied for their ostentatious lives and repeated weddings. Ultimately, they became iconic for their enduring style and influence on popular culture, and even admired for their sass and female independence.

Sarah & Angelina Grimké

First American female advocates
of abolition and women's rights

Sarah (1792–1873)
Angelina (1805–1879)

Sarah and Angelina had a strong bond from the start, even though there were thirteen years between them. Sarah became a godmother as well as a sister when Angelina was born. Angelina sometimes even called her Mother, even though they were sisters. From then on, their lives were intertwined.

Originally from Charleston, South Carolina, the sisters grew up with twelve other siblings, surrounded by plantations, in an aristocratic family that owned slaves. Sarah was appalled by the treatment and suffering of the enslaved people, and secretly taught Hetty, an enslaved house servant, how to read. Sarah felt alone in her convictions though, and she wanted a different life. So when she grew up, she moved north to Philadelphia, where slavery was illegal, and converted to Quakerism, a religion with antislavery principles.Though far apart, the sisters stayed in touch, and eight years later, Angelina moved to Philadelphia to be close to her sister and help with her abolitionist mission. Later, at Angelina's wedding to one of America's most prominent abolitionist activists, Theodore Weld, they had a white and Black minister lead services together.

In Philadelphia, the sisters became involved in the antislavery movement. They wrote letters back home, imploring people to join the abolition cause. They gave public speeches against slavery. Angelina was a particularly mesmerizing speaker. The sisters usually spoke together, but sometimes their audience was so huge, they

had to split up the crowd. Some of their audiences were called "promiscuous," at that time, meaning they included men as well as women. Many of the men were shocked that women were lecturing!

These bold moves made the Grimké sisters very unpopular in the South. They were criticized by many, not only for being abolitionists but also because they were women who dared speak their minds in public. As a response, in 1838, Sarah published *Letters on the Equality of the Sexes*, where she discussed the causes of women's inequality and proposed possible solutions. It was totally radical at the time! And so, the Grimké sisters took on advocating for women's rights as well and befriended other activists, like Elizabeth Cady Stanton. In the same year, Angelina became the first woman in United States history to speak in front of lawmakers when she spoke at the State House in Boston and delivered an antislavery petition signed by twenty thousand Massachusetts women. (At the time, petitions to Congress had become a popular political action that women could take, as voting and getting elected were prohibited to them.) Angelina famously asked, "Are we aliens because we are women? . . . Have women no country?" The Grimké sisters are remembered as the first American women to speak publicly against slavery, and in many ways the first to launch the public discussion for equal rights for women.

Kamala & Maya Harris

US senator and vice president,
and civil rights lawyer

Kamala Devi (born 1964)
Maya Lakshmi (born 1967)

Kamala and Maya are a powerhouse pair! As toddlers, they marched with their parents in civil rights protests. They were always encouraged to be political and take action for causes they cared about.

Kamala and Maya grew up in Oakland, California, and were raised in a multicultural family. Their mother was a scientist from India, and their father an economist from Jamaica. Their home was always full of music, dance, and good food. The sisters' names both have Indian roots. Kamala means "lotus" in Hindi and is another name for the Hindu goddess Lakshmi. Maya is also the name of a Hindu goddess, Durga. Both symbolize the strength and empowerment of women.

As children, Kamala and Maya visited India often. The sisters were inspired by their grandfather, a politician, and their grandmother, who was a women's rights activist. They also visited their family and cousins in Jamaica.

But things changed when the sisters were very young. Their parents divorced, and the girls were raised mostly by their mother, who was a big influence in their lives. She brought them up to be strong women who are proud of their heritages. And she taught them to always stand up for what they believed. The divorce brought Kamala and Maya even closer together, and to this day they are each other's biggest supporters.

In middle school, Kamala and Maya moved to Montreal, Canada, with their mother for her new job. There, they dipped their toes into activism and politics themselves. In the apartment complex where they lived, there was an empty courtyard that was closed for residents. Kamala organized other kids to join her and  Maya in a campaign. The goal: to convince the owner to convert the empty space into a playground for the neighborhood kids. The results: the owner agreed! The sisters' very first campaign was a success!

As adults, both Kamala and Maya went on to become lawyers. Throughout their careers, they remained engaged in public policy, civil rights, and social activism. Maya worked as a law professor and became a leader at the American Civil Liberties Union (the ACLU), which fights for equal rights. She also became a political analyst for different organizations and on television.

Kamala aspired to serve in public office, and she achieved many firsts: she worked as San Francisco's district attorney and later became the attorney general of California—the first woman AND the first person of color in both positions. And in 2016, Kamala was elected as US senator for California, which made her the first South Asian–American senator ever!

In 2019, Kamala ran in the democratic primaries for president, while Maya served as the chair of her campaign. Kamala calls Maya the smartest person she knows and consults her on many issues. Kamala went on to become the first woman of color to be on a major party's ticket as vice president. And in 2020, she became the first woman *and* first woman of color to be elected vice president! This powerhouse pair of sisters is going places!

Anna & Emma Hyers

American singers and pioneers
of Black musical theater

Anna (1855–1925)
Emma (1857–1899)

From a young age, everyone could see that Anna and Emma were extremely talented. They both studied piano and took voice lessons at the encouragement of their father, Sam Hyers (who later managed their whole musical career). Together, the musical sisters started to perform at private house parties and got comfortable singing in front of audiences. When they were only nine and eleven years old, they performed in Sacramento's Metropolitan theater in California for eight hundred people!

After that big performance, the sisters took a break from the stage for five years and worked on perfecting their craft. In 1869, they started to perform again, this time in Boston, Massachusetts, to rave reviews. One critic wrote, "They are without a doubt, destined to occupy a high position in the musical world." And they were! In 1871, the sisters were ready to perform nationally, and they began touring all over the United States for white and Black audiences with their troupe, called "the Colored Operatic and Dramatic Company." At that time, people weren't used to seeing Black women perform opera. The Hyers sisters quickly became celebrities, and they were the first African American women to succeed as concert artists. The sisters got fabulous reviews everywhere they went. The audiences loved them! By now, they were performing in front of as many as five thousand people at a time.

Later in their careers, Anna and Emma ventured into theater as well, and that's when they really made a mark on performance art history. The sisters began to produce innovative musical plays about the Black experience. Their first production was called *Out of Bondage*, and it depicted Black history from slavery to freedom.

The sisters' performances were different and unlike any other musicals of their time. They were a medley of styles and influences, and they included authentic African American dances, plantation songs, opera, and ballads. Not only did they have a storyline and characters, but they discussed the complex experience of Black people in America, including the terrible conditions of being enslaved and the path to freedom. Until that time, Black performers never spoke about slavery and only performed music that was self-deprecating, silly, or humorous. Anna and Emma changed that: they created the first civil rights musicals, with an attempt to create new paradigms of Black identity postslavery. As such, their plays became part of a resistance movement against racism. The sisters created a brand-new kind of African American theater, which empowered Black people and gave them a voice.

Norah Jones & Anoushka Shankar

American and Indian singers

Norah (born 1979)
Anoushka (born 1981)

Sisters Norah Jones and Anoushka Shankar only met in 1997, when they were teenagers.

Norah grew up in Texas, while Anoushka lived in London, England, and in Delhi, India.

However, their lives, though thousands of miles apart, had many similarities: they both had the same world-famous father, the Indian classical musician Ravi Shankar, who influenced them deeply. And both Anoushka and Norah grew up to become world-famous accomplished musicians in their own right.

Anoushka and Norah both loved music from a young age. Norah sang in the church choir and took piano lessons. In her performing arts high school, she won a student music award for Best Jazz Vocalist. Norah went on to study jazz piano at the University of North Texas but left after two years to pursue her music career as a singer and songwriter in New York City.

She was soon successful; she signed with Blue Note Records and released her mega-hit debut solo album, *Come Away with Me*, in 2002. Her music has been described as a combination of sophisticated jazz with the sensibility of Californian singer-songwriters from the 1970s. The album won her five Grammy awards, and sold eighteen million copies worldwide! Since then, Norah has gone on

to make seven more albums on her own, as well as several collaborations, which won her much acclaim and more Grammys.

Meanwhile, on the other side of the ocean, Anoushka had learned sitar (a classical Indian instrument) with her father from the age of nine. She began performing as a classical sitarist when she was only thirteen. Growing up, Anoushka knew George Harrison (the famous guitarist from the Beatles), who was a close friend of her father's. In 2005, she released her album *Rise*, which was nominated for a Grammy Award. As a result of this nomination, Anoushka became the first ever Indian artist to perform at the Grammy Awards. With her music, she is experimental and innovative. She bridges genres and cultures, as she mixes classical Indian music with music from around the world.

In 2013, the sisters collaborated for the first time on an album, *Traces of You*. For the album, Anoushka played sitar, while Norah contributed vocals to three of the songs. The sisters, who usually play very different music, felt that working together brought them closer as sisters too.

The Kardashian/ Jenner Sisters

Kourtney, Kim & Khloé Kardashian and Kendall & Kylie Jenner

Kourtney (born 1979), Kim (born 1980), Khloé (born 1984),
Kendall (born 1995), Kylie (born 1997)

The Kardashian sisters were basically born famous.

Their father, Robert Kardashian, was a lawyer who in 1995 defended football player O. J. Simpson in his notorious and controversial murder trial in Los Angeles. Although Robert was divorced at the time of the trial, his ex-wife Kris (later nicknamed "Momager" for managing her daughters) and their four children—Kim, Kourtney, Khloé, and Robert Jr.—were thrown into the spotlight due to Robert's fame. But there was more. At the time, Kris was married to Caitlyn Jenner, who was famous for being an Olympic champion—winning the gold medal in the men's decathlon in the 1976 Montreal Olympic Games—and who also had four children. Together, Kris and Caitlyn had two more daughters: Kendall and Kylie. The kids grew up in the limelight and with much media attention.

Their fame became even more pronounced when, in 2007, the combined Kardashian/Jenner family began starring in a reality TV show called *Keeping Up with the Kardashians*, which documented the family's life and produced multiple spin-offs. The show portrayed a lot of drama and fights between the sisters, though it was hard to discern what was real and what was staged. In one season, for example, the sisters were shown going to dramatic therapy sessions together in order to better communicate with each other. *Keeping Up with the Kardashians* became a huge hit, though it has also been widely criticized as promoting the concept of "famous for being famous."

♡ 3,759,426

The Kardashians made headlines once again in 2015, when Kris and Caitlyn Jenner got divorced. That same year, Caitlyn came out as a transgender woman. This only stoked the Kardashian fame flame.

Besides being TV celebs, all five sisters are style icons and social media influencers: Kim is probably the best known of the sisters; she's especially famous for her selfies. In 2018, she played a key role in the release of a woman from prison, and since then she decided she wants to become a lawyer like her father and fight for social justice. Kourtney and Khloé are involved in different fashion and fragrance ventures and endorse products on social media. Kendall is a top model and has a successful career, appearing in campaigns of top fashion houses such as Louis Vuitton, Chanel, and Prada. Unlike her older sisters, Kendall mostly keeps her life private and travels a lot. Kylie is a model, a media personality, and an entrepreneur. She founded the successful beauty product company Kylie Cosmetics in 2015 when she was only eighteen years old! She was also included in the prestigious Forbes 2020 list of America's Self-Made Women.

Beyoncé & Solange Knowles

Pop stars, artists, musicians

Beyoncé (born 1981)
Solange (born 1986)

Not many sisters are known by monotyms—or by their first names alone. Hello, Beyoncé and Solange.

Beyoncé has reached super fame and is basically a household name around the world. Named "Queen B/Bey" by her fans, she is one of the most successful pop singers ever. Her younger sister, Solange, may be a bit less known, but she is an accomplished musician in her own right and has won numerous awards for her music and performances. Beyoncé and Solange broke a world record in 2016 by being the first sisters to both have their albums reach No. 1 on the Billboard chart.

The sisters were born in Texas to an African American father, Mathew Knowles (who later would become their manager), and a mother of Creole descent, Tina Lawson (who taught her daughters to always be in control of their image and voice). The sisters both studied music, dance, and theater as children, and fell in love with performing. Beyoncé won a talent show when she was seven and began to perform in a singing/rapping girls group around Texas and, later, on national TV. This group eventually became Destiny's Child, an R & B group that hit No. 1 on the charts. For most of her life, Beyoncé was meticulously groomed and branded to become a megastar.

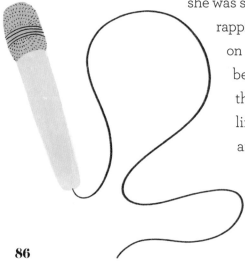

At times, Solange felt overshadowed by her successful big sister.

But she was always encouraged by her mother, who made sure both she and Beyoncé went to therapy so they could process all the fame and stress in a healthy way. Solange began writing her own songs when she was nine. When she was fourteen she danced for Beyoncé's group, Destiny's Child. (Kelly Rowland, one of the group members, was injured, and Solange filled in for her.) When she was seventeen she was part of a jazz band.

The sisters both eventually became multitalented solo artists with strong personal creative visions. Beyoncé creates a whole visual language in her performances and public images, referencing art history and Black culture. She mixes fashion, art, and music to create an artistic experience. Solange has many talents too; beyond writing, singing, and producing her albums, she makes sculptures, digital art, and performance pieces, which are exhibited in prestigious museums worldwide. She was named the Harvard Foundation Artist of the Year in 2018. Both Beyoncé and Solange, who are close supporters of each other's work, discuss issues such as body image, race, and Black womanhood in their songs and performances. Each sister is considered a fierce trailblazer and innovator in the music industry.

Ann Landers &
Dear Abby

Famous American advice columnists

Ann Landers, a.k.a. Esther "Eppie" (1918–2002)
Dear Abby, a.k.a. Pauline "Popo" (1918–2013)

Pauline
(Dear Abby)

Esther
(Ann Landers)

Esther Pauline (Eppie) and Pauline Esther (Popo) were identical twins born seventeen minutes apart. They talked alike, dressed alike, and slept in the same bed. They got married to their husbands in a double wedding ceremony in 1939, while wearing matching dresses and hairstyles.

And they both became famous for their advice columns.

The twins always loved to write, and as college students, they wrote a joint gossip column titled "The Campus Rat," for the *Collegian Reporter*, the student newspaper of Morningside College in Sioux City, Iowa. In 1955, at the age of thirty-seven, Eppie (a homemaker at the time) won a contest to write the existing column Ask Ann Landers for the *Chicago Sun-Times*. In this column, people wrote in questions about everything from proper etiquette to relationships, and Eppie replied with wit and sass. Her column quickly became a smash hit; it was translated into twenty languages and appeared in more than twelve hundred different newspapers.

At first, her twin, Popo (also a homemaker at the time), would offer her opinion too, but the *Chicago Sun-Times* did not approve of this partnership. Popo decided to write a column of her own. In 1956, she began writing "Dear Abby" under the pen name of "Abigail Van Buren" for the *San Francisco Chronicle*. Her column also became a huge hit, and in 1963 Popo began hosting a radio show,

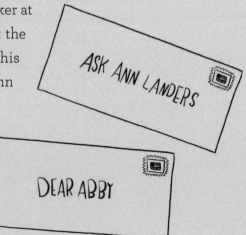

Dear Abby, on CBS Radio. Popo's column and show were rivals to the "Ask Ann Landers" column. Eppie was furious that her sister was competing with her, and this led to a feud between them. The once-inseparable twins didn't speak to each other for almost ten years! They reconciled in 1964, but the tension remained to the end of their lives.

Popo retired from writing "Dear Abby" in 2000, and her daughter, Jeanne, took over the column, which she still writes to this very day. Eppie died in 2002, and her column ended. Her daughter, Margo Howard, writes her own advice column, called "Dear Margo." Sadly, these two cousins are also rivals.

The sisters' columns were known and loved for their straightforward tone and practical advice given as if to a friend. Both used lots of humor and sarcasm, much of which was influenced by their Jewish and Yiddish upbringing. They each offered a fresh new twist over previous advice columns, which were often very serious in tone. In addition, both sisters used their columns to promote their liberal agenda and advocated for gun control, women's rights, and civil rights.

Margaret & Frances MacDonald

Scottish artists who were some of the first to create a new artistic style called Art Nouveau

Margaret (1864–1933)
Frances (1873–1921)

Art Nouveau (which means "new art" in French) is an artistic style that blossomed in Europe between 1890 and 1914. This style can still be seen in many places today: in paintings, architecture, and even home décor and jewelry. It is inspired by the beauty of nature and has lots of long, curvy lines and floral designs. Some important artists associated with this movement include Gustav Klimt and Alphonse Mucha. However, some of the artists behind this style have been forgotten, mainly the women. Two of these women were sisters Margaret and Frances MacDonald from Glasgow, Scotland.

Margaret and Frances grew up in an upper-class family and studied in the modern Glasgow School of Art. There, they met their future husbands, who were artists as well. Together, they were nicknamed "the Glasgow Four." The sisters were inspired by old Celtic traditions and used a lot of symbolism in their work. Their designs had geometrical elements to them and drew from mythology, nature, and science. At the time, the style of their art was considered innovative and modern. In 1896, an article about their work in the journal *Studio* said it was "a very definite and not unsuccessful attempt to create a style of decoration which owes absolutely nothing to the past."

Margaret and Frances were examples of Europe's fin de siècle (end of the nineteenth century) "New Women"—women who sought professions that traditionally were available only to men. In their work, Margaret and Frances

reflected upon their new roles and depicted women who defy normal gender characteristics. They created female figures who appear strong and independent, as opposed to the traditional representation of women as more passive. The sisters' work was sometimes criticized for this untraditional approach, yet today it is considered ground-breaking.

Around 1896, Margaret and Frances opened a shop in Glasgow, where they sold paintings, jewelry, embroidery, glass and metal objects, as well as furniture. They also designed advertisements and posters. The sisters were close, and they worked together on almost all their pieces.

Margaret and Frances had some success during their lifetimes, and they exhibited their art in galleries all around Europe. However, the MacDonald sisters were far from the heart of the Art Nouveau movement, which was in Vienna, Austria. This made it harder for them to become well-known in the field. In addition, researchers think that because they were women, they were not taken as seriously as their husbands, and they were left out of art history. Today, the MacDonald sisters have been rediscovered and are regarded as important in creating the foundation for Art Nouveau and for having influenced the great art masters who came after them.

Tashi & Nungshi Malik

First siblings to climb Mount Everest

Tashi (born 1991)
Nungshi (born 1991)

Tashi

Nungshi

It's hard to tell Tashi and Nungshi apart. Not only are they identical twins, but they also like to dress identically! Their outfits are not ordinary ones though. They include matching hiking pants, huge sunglasses, thick gloves, and heavy boots. This is because the sisters are always on some expedition.

Tashi and Nungshi grew up in Northern India. Their names are actually nicknames given by their father: Tashi is "good luck" in Tibetan, and Nungshi means "love" in Manipuri, but the sisters have adopted them as their official names.

The twins have always shared a passion for the outdoors and a love of sports. As young girls at school, they excelled at hockey, basketball, badminton, and everything athletic. Their father, who has always been their mentor, encouraged them to push and challenge themselves and believed that while living in extreme situations they can develop their leadership skills and become better people as well. The sisters took his words to heart.

When they were eighteen, Tashi and Nungshi discovered mountaineering (everything to do with the challenge of mountain climbing) and went to study at a professional school. After much hard work, and with the encouragement of their teachers, they felt ready to embark on a huge mission: to climb Mount Everest. In preparation, the sisters trained for several years and raised money; they needed about $80,000 for the expedition. Four years later, the twins finally fulfilled their dream and reached the top of Everest, thus becoming the first twins ever to achieve this amazing feat!

Once they reached their goal, the sisters set out for more. This time, their mission was to conquer the Seven Summits, a challenge to climb the highest mountain in each continent, totaling seven peaks. In 2014, they completed this lofty plan, and by doing so they broke the world record as the first twins to do so together. And they did not stop there! In 2015, Tashi and Nungshi traveled to the North and South Poles through extremely tough weather conditions, thus becoming the youngest people ever to complete the "Explorers Grand Slam" (which includes climbing the Seven Summits as well as reaching both the North and South Poles). They were only twenty-three years old at the time! The sisters were also the first South Asians to achieve this accomplishment, and of course they were the first twins to do so. In 2020, the twins participated in the reality TV show the *World's Toughest Race: Eco-Challenge Fiji*. Their team, consisting of five members, came in 35th out of 66.

Tashi and Nungshi see climbing not only as a challenge and as a way to become better people but also as an act in support of gender equality in India. They want to be role models for girls everywhere to follow their dreams. As part of this goal, the twins founded the Nungshi Tashi Foundation, which empowers girls through outdoor leadership.

Susanna & Linda Manziaris

Canadian sisters who build schools and provide scholarships to help destitute girls around the world

Susanna (born 1997)
Linda (born 2000)

Susanna and Linda Manziaris are a power-duo sister team from Canada. When they were only teenagers in high school, they founded a charity that helped many girls around the world.

The idea began when Susanna saw *It's a Girl*, a documentary film about gendercide—the systematic practice of killing young baby girls around the world, just for being girls. According to the UN, more than one hundred million girls have been victims of gendercide to date. Susanna recalls that this movie completely changed her life, and she first felt a need to take action.

Not long after, Susanna and Linda took a family trip to Kenya. The trip made them realize what a difference education can make in the lives of girls. The sisters saw how the girls who attended school got better jobs and had much better living situations than the girls without schooling. Back home from their trip, teenagers Susanna and Linda decided that they want to do their part to promote education and help girls around the world.

Soon their plans became a reality. In 2013, Susanna established the charity GirlsHelpingGirls. The foundation promotes education of women and girls, and through that education, GHG helps them obtain a better future. Her younger sister, Linda, is a designer who started her own jewelry company called Body Bijou. Linda helped start the GHG foundation by donating $15,000 from her designs, and to this day the company donates fifty percent of their income to the charity.

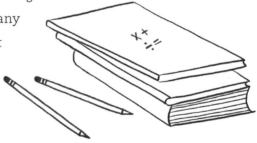

The sister team, through the GHG Foundation, was successful in raising $120,000 by selling buttons and holding donation campaigns at their school. With the funds, they were able to provide scholarships to many girls in South Africa, Afghanistan, and Haiti who wouldn't be able to study otherwise. In addition, the foundation built three schools in Jamaica and founded a teacher training program in Afghanistan.

The industrious sisters also promote entrepreneurship for young people. In 2014, Linda won the Young Entrepreneur of the Year at the Startup Canada Awards, when she was only fourteen years old.

In 2017, Susanna and Linda were honored by the Greek America Foundation at the Gabby Awards at Carnegie Hall. Gabby stands for Greek America's Best and Brightest, and according to their website: "The awards honor those North American individuals who strive for excellence in their careers, philanthropic life, and in the service of the public."

Hannah &
Tatyana McFadden

Paralympic athletes

Tatyana (born 1989)
Hannah (born 1996)

Tatyana

Hannah

Sisters Hannah and Tatyana loved to race one another since they were young girls. But their races were extra fast; both sisters use a wheelchair.

Tatyana, adopted from a Russian orphanage as a child, is paralyzed from the waist down and had to walk on her hands until the age of six. Her younger sister, Hannah, who was adopted from Albania, has one leg amputated above the knee.

Hannah and Tatyana (nicknamed "the Beast" because of her strength and drive) grew up in Maryland with two moms, Debbie McFadden and Bridget O'Shaughnessey, and a younger sister, Ruthi. Debbie became an advocate for disabled people after being paralyzed herself for eight years. In 1989, she was appointed by President George H. W. Bush as the US commissioner of disabilities. In her role, Debbie helped write the Americans with Disabilities Act of 1990, which prohibits disability-based discrimination. She and Bridget raised their daughters to believe they can do anything they set their minds to, no matter what physical impairments they have.

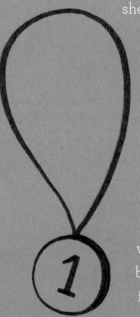

Growing up, Hannah and Tatyana both loved sports, and they trained together for long hours to become athletes, zipping around the track in racing wheelchairs. In 2012, they finally achieved their dreams: both attended the Olympics in London. This was the first time siblings have competed against each other in the Paralympic Games. They went on to compete also in the Rio De Janeiro Olympics in 2016. So far, Tatyana is a seventeen-time Paralympic medalist in track and field, out of which seven medals are gold!

In 2013, she was the first woman to earn six titles at a single Paralympic championship. Hannah has so far won four bronze medals in various world championships.

These champion sisters did not always have a smooth path, and they met with challenges along the way. When Tatyana was fifteen years old, she wanted to race with her friends at school but was not permitted to do so. She filed a lawsuit against her high school, and after several years she finally won the battle. Her lawsuit had a huge national impact, and in 2013 the US Department of Education's Office of Civil Rights issued a letter requiring schools to provide equal access to all activities. This experience paved the way for Hannah and Tatyana to become advocates for Paralympic athletes, who are not treated equally to able-bodied athletes. For instance, the Olympic Committee grants $25,000 to Americans who win an Olympic gold. However, they award only $5,000 for every Paralympic gold medalist. The sisters' mission is to change the perception of people with disabilities and fight for their equality.

Kate & Pippa Middleton

English duchess and socialite

Catherine "Kate" (born 1982)
Philippa "Pippa" (born 1983)

Kate and Pippa Middleton live a modern fairy tale.

Their story begins in a village in Berkshire, England. The sisters were born to a family of "commoners," the British term for nonroyals. When they were little, Kate's nickname was Squeak and Pippa's was Pip, named after their school's hamsters (Pippa later earned the nickname "Perfect Pip" because she was excellent at everything). Both sisters loved climbing trees, playing sports, and hiking with Girlguiding (known in the United States as the Girl Scouts). Pippa dreamed of winning the Wimbledon tennis tournament when she grew up; Kate was a star swimmer. Though the sisters were competitive, they always supported each other.

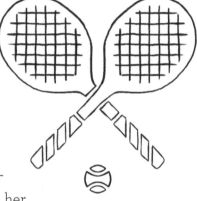

For college, Kate chose to study art history at St. Andrews, the oldest university in Scotland and one of the most prestigious. During her second year, she participated in a charity fashion show sponsored by the French fashion house Yves Saint-Laurent.

That's when British prince William saw her. He was a student there too, and they soon became friends. One thing led to another, and they began dating in 2003.

Like Kate, Pippa attended college in Scotland, where she earned a degree in English literature from the University of Edinburgh. And like her big sister, the popular Pippa hung out with the royal kids of dukes and earls.

After college, Kate and Pippa lived together in London and were well-known because of their connection to royalty. Kate worked for her family's business of party supplies, helping with catalog design and marketing. Pippa worked in event planning and public relations, and she was considered one of England's most eligible bachelorettes. In 2007, Kate and William briefly broke up, and Pippa was there to support her sister.

But Kate's story has a happy ending: she and Prince William wed in 2011, and she became Her Royal Highness the Duchess of Cambridge. Kate is the first "commoner" since the seventeenth century to marry into British royalty and the first future queen with a working background! Kate entered smoothly into her new role and is adored by her grandmother-in-law, Queen Elizabeth II. Since her wedding to Prince William, Kate does charity work in support of children, mental health, and art.

The royal wedding also shot Pippa into world fame for being Kate's maid of honor. Pippa adores the limelight that comes with being the future queen's sister. She is married to former racing driver James Matthews and writes columns for publications such as *Vanity Fair* about traditional English pursuits as well as sports. She also published a party-planning book called *Celebrate: A Year of Festivities for Families and Friends*. Like Kate, Pippa advocates for causes that are important to her, such as the British Heart Foundation, where she promotes a healthy lifestyle for women.

Kate and Pippa are both style icons and are frequently named "best dressed" in the media. The sisters still love tennis, and the two can be seen at Wimbledon every year!

Patria, Minerva, María Teresa & Dedé Mirabal

Dominican sisters who opposed
the dictatorship

Patria (1924–1960), Dedé (1925–2014),
Minerva (1926–1960), María Teresa (1935–1960)

The Mirabal sisters were called "Las Mariposas"—the butterflies. This was not just an ordinary nickname. This was their secret underground name.

The four sisters grew up in the Dominican Republic in 1930, during a harsh dictatorship, led by General Rafael Leónidas Trujillo (a.k.a. El Jefe, or "the Boss" in Spanish). Patria, Minerva, and María Teresa attended university at a time when not many women did so. (Dedé stayed at home to help run the family business.) At a student party, Minerva had an extremely unpleasant encounter with Trujillo, which ended with Minerva slapping him across the face. He continued to harass her family as a result. Patria, Minerva, and María Teresa decided they must do something to end his reign of terror (which included kidnappings, disappearances, murders, and rapes, and other terrible behavior).

The sisters, along with their husbands, secretly made a plan to sabotage the regime and assassinate Trujillo. Together, they formed a resistance group against the dictatorship called the Movement of the Fourteenth of June, named for the day in 1959 when a huge massacre took place. The sisters' code name, "Las Mariposas," was a sign of hope and transformation. They knew it was extremely dangerous, but they were willing to take the risk for the sake of their country's future. Patria said, "We cannot allow our children to grow up in this corrupt and tyrannical regime. We have to

North Atlantic Ocean

Dominican Republic

Carribean Sea

fight against it, and I am willing to give up everything, even my life if necessary."

When Trujillo realized what was happening, he incarcerated the sisters and other members of the group, but this did not stop their fight. They continued their resistance from jail until their release in 1960. Tragically, that same year, Patria, Minerva, and María Teresa were murdered by Trujillo's regime. The sisters were on their way to see their husbands in prison, and the assassination was made to look like a car accident. Their deaths caused rage and shock among Dominican women, and they mobilized the resistance group to fight harder. The escalation worked; Trujillo himself was finally assassinated in 1961, bringing an end to the dictatorship in the Dominican Republic.

Dedé, the fourth sister, survived, and raised the remaining six children of her sisters. She also founded the Mirabal Sisters Foundation to keep their memory alive.

Today, the sisters are seen as icons of feminist resistance. Las Mariposas have been commemorated in popular culture, such as in books and films, and appear on a two-hundred-pesos bill in the Dominican Republic. In 1999, the United Nations dedicated November 25, the day of the sisters' death, as the International Day for the Elimination of Violence Against Women in honor of the brave Butterflies.

Kate & Laura Mulleavy

American fashion designers

Katherine "Kate" (born 1979)
Laura (born 1980)

Kate and Laura are the powerhouse team of sisters behind one of the most important American fashion houses, Rodarte. The sisters, who are close in age, grew up in Northern California. Their mother, Victoria Rodart, is an artist of Mexican-Italian descent, and their father is a mycologist, which means he studies mushrooms. Their grandmother was an opera singer, and the sisters were fascinated by her elaborate stage costumes. Growing up, the girls spent a lot of time outdoors, but they also watched a lot of old films, which their mother believed was crucial for their artistic education. And indeed, their interest in fashion grew from films such as *Gone with the Wind*.

Neither Kate nor Laura actually studied fashion design officially; they only knew some basic sewing skills from their mother. In college at Berkeley, Laura studied English literature, and Kate studied art history. Because of this, they've been called "outsider nerds" to the fashion world. But the sisters don't mind. They feel that being on the outside gives them their unique avant-garde perspective, which has been described as one that explores "the dark undercurrents of prettiness."

"We don't know anything about what we're doing but our instincts," Kate said in an interview for the *New Yorker*.

Laura and Kate both love nature and often use natural inspirations in their clothes, with elements such as birds

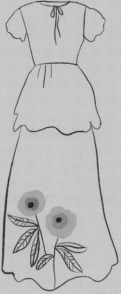

and forests—and yes, mushrooms!—featured in their clothes. They also love horror films and art history, themes that appear in their designs as well.

The two sisters launched their first collection in 2005 while living in Los Angeles. They named it Rodarte after the original Spanish spelling of their mother's maiden name. Their collection, which was featured on the cover of *Women's Wear Daily* (a fashion industry journal, named "the Bible of fashion") caught the attention of the famous *Vogue* editor Anna Wintour, who flew out to California to meet with them. The sisters were very new to the industry at the time, but the meeting with Anna launched their career. She told them to keep making their clothes personal. This was the advice they needed to hear! Since then, their clothing lines have been sold internationally and worn by many famous women, including Michelle Obama, Nicole Kidman, Lady Gaga, and Beyoncé.

The Mulleavy sisters see their designs as art, and they designed costumes for the film *Black Swan* in 2010. They love designing costumes for characters, and did so also for the LA Philharmonic performance of the opera *Don Giovanni* from 2012, which they were particularly excited about because of their grandmother's connection to opera. Their work has been exhibited in multiple museums and has won many awards.

Recently, the artistic sisters have also ventured into filmmaking, with their debut movie, *Woodshock*. They cowrote and directed the film, which starred Kirsten Dunst and came out in 2017.

Malia & Sasha Obama

First Daughters of President Barack Obama
and First Lady Michelle Obama

Malia (born 1998)
Natasha "Sasha" (born 2001)

Malia (nicknamed "Little Potato" by her mom) and Natasha (everyone calls her Sasha) were born in Chicago, Illinois. However, they spent a lot of their childhood in one of the most famous houses in the world—the White House—with their dad, the forty-fourth US president, Barack Obama, and their mom, First Lady Michelle Obama.

Before his inauguration, their dad wrote an open letter with big wishes for them "to grow up in a world with no limits on your dreams and no achievements beyond your reach, and to grow into compassionate, committed women who will help build that world."

Growing up in the White House and in the spotlight sounds super glamorous, but their parents tried to give the sisters as normal a life as possible. As their mom said: "For eight years, we were like, 'Yup, your dad's president.' That doesn't have anything to do with you. Take your butt to school." But in reality, did the sisters have normal childhoods? Not entirely. For example, the sisters had to have security all the time, to which their mom said, "Yes, you have security, just ignore them; they're not here for you." Easier said than done! Speaking of security, in the White House, everyone had code names: Malia's code name was Radiance (because she loves Raisin Bran), and Sasha's was Rosebud (a famous last word from the movie *Citizen Kane*, which she loves).

As children, Malia and Sasha kept busy; both had dance, tennis, and piano lessons, among other activities. Like everyone else, they had to do their chores (like making their beds and setting the table) and had slumber parties (imagine being invited to one at the White House!). They even had a tree house. The sisters also took care of pets; before their big move to Washington, DC, their dad promised they could adopt a puppy at their new home. They adopted Bo first and then Sunny—both Portuguese water dogs.

As teenagers, the sisters continued to lead a busy life. Malia excelled in sports—in basketball, tennis, and volleyball (she won four volleyball championships, three basketball titles, and multiple championships in tennis) and, like her dad, took on leadership roles (she was senior class president in high school). Sasha worked at a seafood restaurant at Martha's Vineyard during her high school summer break. Both sisters have become style icons too, and in 2014, *Time* magazine listed them as two of "The 25 Most Influential Teens of 2014"!

In addition to all their activities, Malia and Sasha participated in some of their mom's philanthropic efforts. In 2016, the sisters traveled with their mom and their grandmother, Marian Robinson, to Liberia, Morocco, and Spain to promote the "Let Girls Learn Peace Initiative," in support of girls' education around the world.

As they got older, each sister focused on her own interests. Malia, who is keen on TV and film, worked at different studios in New York and Los Angeles. And before starting college, she took a gap year and traveled to Bolivia and Peru for eighty-three days (her Spanish is excellent!). She enrolled at Harvard in 2017, majoring in visual and environmental studies. Sasha, in turn, began her college studies at the University of Michigan in 2019, where she is on the dance team. Big sister Malia helped Sasha move into college! As you can imagine, the college dorms where the sisters live are quite different from their rooms at the White House. And yet, as daughters of a former president, even in college, Malia and Sasha always have secret security not far behind!

Mary-Kate, Ashley & Elizabeth Olsen

Actors, designers, and entrepreneurs

Ashley (born 1986)
Mary-Kate (born 1986)
Elizabeth (born 1989)

HOLLYWOOD

Ashley

Elizabeth

Mary-Kate

Many people remember Michelle Tanner, the supercute baby (and eventually toddler and little kid) from *Full House*, a sitcom that ran from 1987 to 1995. Well, that baby was actually played by two babies—twins Mary-Kate and Ashley Olsen. They took turns playing Michelle in order to comply with child labor laws. Fun fact—Ashley and Mary-Kate are not identical; they are actually fraternal twins! And another fact from the set: when the twins got older and started losing teeth, they often had to wear fake ones so Michelle would look consistent!

Growing up, Ashley and Mary-Kate continued to perform on TV and in film projects. This made them some of the wealthiest sisters in the entertainment industry. And though they grew up in glamour, the twins remember their childhoods as challenging sometimes: they had to take on adult responsibilities from a young age, and their private lives were constantly in the spotlight for everyone to see. In addition, as a result of playing Michelle, they were often seen as one entity. These childhood experiences shaped the rest of the twins' lives. As adults they are determined to carve out their own identities, and they both fiercely guard their privacy. More than anything, they long to break free of their image as childhood celebrities.

Ashley and Mary-Kate have a younger sister, Elizabeth. (They also have an older brother and two younger half siblings, from their father's second marriage.) When Elizabeth (sometimes called Lizzie) was young, she occasionally costarred with Mary-Kate and Ashley on-screen, but as she got older, she was keen to carve out her own path. In high

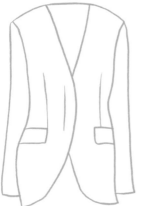

school, Elizabeth unofficially adopted her middle name Chase as her last name, so she could stay under the radar. In college, she studied acting at NYU in New York City and also in Moscow, Russia! Elizabeth went on to become an award-winning Hollywood actress in her own right, as well as a producer. She currently stars in many popular movies to international acclaim.

Her older sisters, however, shifted their attention away from acting. Ashley and Mary-Kate became interested in fashion and design as well as entrepreneurship. For a while they were the face of the fashion house Badgley Mischka and later launched a luxury fashion label, the Row, which is highly regarded for its impeccable details and tailoring. They also created a more affordable label, Elizabeth and James—named for their siblings! Ashley and Mary-Kate were named Womenswear Designer of the Year by the Council of Fashion Designers of America (CFDA) in 2012 as well as in 2015. The twins were also praised for supporting workers' rights by making a pledge to allow maternity leave for their workers in Bangladesh. Nowadays, Ashley and Mary-Kate's mission is to create beautiful fashion that is not clouded by their past Hollywood careers but speaks for itself.

Margaret & Matilda Roumania Peters, a.k.a. "Pete" and "Repeat"

American tennis players

Margaret (1915–2004)
Matilda Roumania (1917–2003)

Like many kids, sisters Margaret and Matilda Roumania played tennis for fun. But unlike other kids, the sisters saw tennis as more than a hobby; by the time they were teenagers, they began to play competitively.

Margaret and Matilda Roumania grew up near Washington, DC, and played tennis in Rose Park, across from their home. They were always very close. Margaret, who was two years older, waited for Matilda Roumania to graduate from high school so they could enroll in college at the same time. The college, Tuskegee University (a historically Black university in Tuskegee, Alabama) gave the two sisters each a four-year scholarship to play tennis for their team. The sisters both graduated with physical education degrees.

After college, Margaret and Matilda Roumania continued to compete in tennis matches. At that time, sports in America were segregated: African Americans were not allowed to compete against Caucasian Americans. So the Peters sisters, who were nicknamed "Pete" and "Repeat," played with the American Tennis Association (ATA), which was created specially to give Black people a place to play tennis competitively, and is the oldest Black sports organization in America. The sisters had to pay for their own equipment, gear, and travel, as there was no money available for players in the ATA. To support themselves, the sisters worked throughout their lives as educators.

The Peters sisters quickly became tennis stars and dazzled their audiences. They were feared by their opponents for their outstanding slice serves (a tennis move that keeps the ball low to the ground), chop shots (an aim at the ball made with a downward motion), and strong backhands. Together, the duo won fourteen doubles titles between 1938 and 1953, breaking all records at the time.

Margaret and Matilda Roumania were inducted into the United States Tennis Association (USTA) Mid-Atlantic Section Hall of Fame in 2003. The USTA was the same organization that denied African Americans a chance to compete during most of the sisters' careers. After so many years, the organization finally recognized their outstanding achievements. The sisters were also inducted into the Black Tennis Hall of Fame in 2012.

Margaret and Matilda Roumania were the first sister pair to change the face of tennis for women and paved the way for female stars today.

Stefania & Helena Podgórska

Polish sisters who saved Jews during World War II

Stefania (1925–2018)
Helena (born 1935)

Stefania and Helena, two Polish sisters who were raised Catholic, had a secret. They were hiding thirteen Jews in their tiny attic, with no running water. It was 1942, the height of World War II, and the Germans were occupying Poland. Jews were in grave danger, and times were harsh. Throughout this time, the sisters were on their own: their father had died before the war, and their mother was taken to a German labor camp. So Stefania, who was only seventeen years old, had to take care of her younger sister, ten years her junior. And through all this, they bravely hid Jews.

The Podgórska sisters' story began when Stefania, who grew up on a farm, longed to live in the big city. When she was old enough, she moved to the city of Przemyśl to work for the Jewish Diamant family, who owned a shop. Mrs. Diamant especially loved Stefania, and she treated her like her own daughter.

When the war began, the Diamants and the rest of the Jews were forced to move to a ghetto—a closed neighborhood that was designated only for Jews, with harsh living conditions. From there, many were deported to concentration camps. Stefania began to help her beloved employers by smuggling food into the ghetto. Then, she took in the two Diamant brothers to live secretly in her attic (one of whom later became her husband!). The Diamant brothers convinced Stefania to take in more Jews, until she was hiding thirteen in total.

For two years, the courageous sisters kept the hiders safe. It was very dangerous. On a daily basis, Stefania and Helena had to smuggle enough food to keep everyone alive without looking suspicious to their neighbors. Helena was only seven, and it was easier for a child to sneak around without raising suspicion. Stefania worked in a factory in order to provide for everyone. The women hiding in the attic helped out by knitting articles of clothing, which the sisters sold to make more money. Stefania had to be especially careful: many boys were interested in dating her, but she kept telling them to wait until after the war. She didn't want to risk anyone knowing her secret.

When the Russians liberated Poland in 1944, the thirteen Jews scattered all over the globe. Stefania and her husband, Josef, immigrated to Israel and later to the United States. Stefania stayed in Poland and became a doctor.

In 1979, the Podgórska sisters were honored by the State of Israel as "Righteous Among the Nations" for risking their own lives to save the lives of Jews.

Diana Ross & Barbara Ross-Lee

Record-breaking pop singer and physician

Barbara (born 1942)
Diana (born 1944)

From a young age, sisters Barbara "Bobbi" and Diana "Diane" were clever, creative, and ambitious. Diana loved to perform and be the center of attention, while Barbara was teased for always having a book in her hand.

The sisters had a comfortable childhood, but it was not without hardship. Their mother was very sick for a time, and they were well aware of the racism and segregation in the world around them. Yet both Barbara and Diana have fond memories of growing up surrounded by music. Whether singing at home, in the church choir, performing in plays, or grooving with friends in their neighborhood, music was everywhere!

When Diana was fifteen, she was invited to join a girls' music group called the Primettes. She did not know it at the time, but this moment would change her life. Diana spent all her time with the group, singing and touring. In addition to being the lead singer, the multitalented Diana was also their costume designer, seamstress, makeup artist, and hairstylist!

The Primettes, later renamed the Supremes, went on to become one of the top all-female vocal groups in US history. Eventually, Diana stepped out to form a solo career of her own. She was a huge success, with her songs topping the charts, breaking records, and earning multiple awards. Diana became a legendary pop star, an actress, and a music icon.

Meanwhile, Barbara's interests were quite different from Diana's. Yet she, too, became a star in her own right, in an entirely different field: medicine!

At first, Barbara was discouraged from attending medical school by her college adviser, who thought women shouldn't be physicians. Disappointed but determined, she went on to study chemistry and biology instead. And when she heard of a new osteopathic medical school in Michigan, Barbara immediately enrolled as the only Black woman in her class. To fund her studies and her dream, she sold her house and moved in with her mother, while herself a single mom.

As a physician, Barbara opened her own family practice. She went on to become a professor, and in 1993, she was elected as the first African American woman in the United States to serve as a medical school dean! In that role, she cared deeply about training physicians to be empathic caregivers, who see their patients as people first. She also buckled down on making it easier for people of color and other minorities to enter the medical field. For her contributions to women's health and leadership, Barbara received multiple awards.

Though Barbara and Diana chose very different paths and have led very different lives, their relationship became closer over the years. Ultimately, the sisters shared the experience of following their passions, achieving excellence, and working hard to make a difference in the world.

Angelica, Eliza & Peggy Schuyler

Prominent in the American Revolution

Angelica (1756–1814), Elizabeth "Eliza" (1757–1854),
Margarita "Peggy" (1758–1801)

Eliza

Angelica

Peggy

Y ou may have heard of a very famous man named Alexander Hamilton, who was a founding father of the United States. But chances are you are not familiar with his wife, Elizabeth "Eliza" Schuyler, nor with her two sisters, Peggy and Angelica. Being married to Hamilton, Elizabeth and her sisters had a front-row seat to key events in the formation of the United States. In those early years, women could not vote or become political leaders themselves. But the three sisters helped the leaders of the Revolution behind the scenes.

Eliza, Angelica, and Peggy were the three eldest daughters of Philip Schuyler, a New York—based Revolutionary War general. Their family was considered American royalty. They attended many political events and were friends with prominent figures. For instance, Angelica was invited to George Washington's presidential inauguration in 1789. Charming as well as politically savvy, Angelica befriended and corresponded with other politicians, including Benjamin Franklin, Thomas Jefferson, and her brother-in-law, Alexander Hamilton. (Some speculated that Angelica was secretly in love with Hamilton, while others claimed that their correspondence was merely familial and friendly.) Angelica lived in Europe for a while and held gatherings called "salons," where high society met to discuss the politics of the day. Later, she helped refugees from the French Revolution find a home in America.

Eliza, the second daughter, preferred to stay out of the public eye. She enjoyed quiet activities, such as sewing and gardening. Eliza assisted her husband, Alexander, with his political writings and speeches. (Alexander began his career as an aide to George Washington and

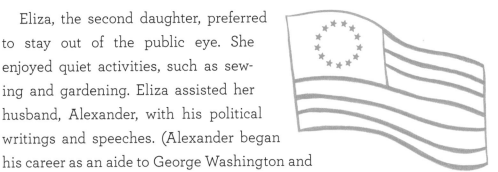

in 1789 became the secretary of the Treasury of the newly formed United States.) Hamilton wrote in a letter to Eliza that she was the "best of wives and best of women." During their life together, Alexander and Eliza had eight children and also fostered a girl, Frances Antill. In 1806, Eliza continued this tradition by helping establish the Orphan Asylum Society, the first private orphanage in New York City. She directed it for over three decades, and it still exists! After Alexander's death, Eliza maintained his legacy and estate. Thanks to her, we know a lot about Hamilton's life today.

Peggy, the third sister, was extremely popular, beautiful, and wickedly witty. She married the Dutch aristocrat Stephen Van Rensselaer III, who until this day is ranked tenth on *Business Insider*'s list of wealthiest Americans of all time. Peggy also had lengthy correspondences with her brother-in-law Hamilton. She died young, leaving her older sisters bereaved.

Today, the story of the Schuyler sisters has been met with renewed interest, thanks to the hit Broadway musical *Hamilton*, which portrays them as behind-the-scenes feminists.

Coretta Scott King & Edythe Scott Bagley

Authors, civil rights leaders, and educators

Edythe (1924–2011)
Coretta (1927–2006)

Coretta Scott King was known as the "First Lady of the Civil Rights Movement." She was the wife of civil rights leader Martin Luther King Jr. (MLK), and together they fought tirelessly for racial equality.

Coretta and her older sister Edythe were born on a farm in Marion, Alabama. The sisters were always best friends and close confidantes. As children, they tended the farm, grew vegetables, and raised chickens, pigs, and cows.

At the time, the Deep South was racially segregated. Black people had to enter through separate doors to go into shops and sit in separate seats on the bus or at the movies. Coretta and Edythe wanted to change this unfair reality. Their parents taught them that education was the key to making this change, and they made sure the sisters attended school every day—even though they had to walk five miles to attend.

Edythe and Coretta took the importance of education to heart. Edythe got a master's degree in English from Columbia University and a master's of fine arts in theater arts from Boston University. She established a theater major at Cheyney University in Philadelphia, Pennsylvania, and taught for twenty-six years. Meanwhile, Coretta, who loved to sing, studied at the New England Conservatory of Music in Boston, Massachusetts. That's where she met Martin Luther King Jr. and decided to marry him, even though that would mean giving up her music career. She helped her husband fight for civil rights through educating the people. She even found a way to incorporate music in their campaigns; she gave concerts to support equality, often with famous musicians such as the composer Duke Ellington.

Coretta and Edythe had front-row seats to the civil rights activism led by MLK. When he was imprisoned in 1960 for refusing to leave a white-only institution, John F. Kennedy, who was campaigning for the presidency at the time, personally called Coretta to offer his sympathy. Soon after, Robert F. Kennedy, the president's brother (and soon to be appointed the US attorney general) was able to help release MLK from prison. People believe that these actions helped mobilize Black people to vote for JFK, who ultimately won the election. Tragically, MLK  was assassinated in 1968 for his outspoken anti-racist activism. Following his death, Edythe moved to Atlanta to support Coretta, and she stayed with her for two years. During that time, the sisters built the King Center for Nonviolent Social Change, in commemoration of MLK and his vision. The sisters continued their involvement in the civil rights movement, and they supported the feminist movement and other human rights causes as well. Edythe often represented Coretta as a speaker and made media appearances on behalf of the Martin Luther King Jr. center. Both sisters ensured that MLK's legacy would be heard all over the world.

Ai-ling, Qing-ling & Mei-ling Soong

Influenced Chinese history in the twentieth century

Ai-Ling (1890–1973), Qing-ling (1892–1981),
Mei-ling (1897–2003)

"One loved money, one loved China, one loved power."
— Maoist saying

Ai-ling

Qing-ling

Mei-ling

In China during the 1800s, it was very difficult for women to have political power. One of the only ways for women to have political and social influence was by marrying. And that's exactly what the Soong sisters did.

The three Soong sisters were born in Shanghai to a well-regarded family. Their mother, Ni Kwei-tseng, was a descendant of a famous mathematician from the Ming dynasty. Their father, Charlie Soong, was a wealthy Methodist minister—one of the few Christians in China at the time. He believed that women should be educated and sent his three daughters to Wesleyan and Wellesley colleges in the United States. This was rare at the time; women in China were usually married off without receiving higher education. In America, the sisters took on English names: Ai-Ling was Nancy, Qing-Ling was Rosamonde, and Mai-ling was May-ling. The three quickly learned English and became well versed in Western culture and technology. These skills contributed to their power later on and enabled them to communicate with foreign governments, unlike most Chinese leaders.

After completing college, all three sisters returned to China and married Chinese politicians. Ai-ling, the oldest, married the rich finance minister H. H. Kung and made investments with their money. At one point she was among the richest women in China! The second daughter, Qing-ling, married the nationalist Sun Yat-sen, who would become the president of China. She was his constant companion and adviser, and in many ways she was the first "first lady" of China. The third sister, Mei-ling, eventually married Sun Yat-sen's successor, Chiang Kai-shek, a military man who set out on a mission to conquer China. Mei-ling supported him and acted as an ambassador of China to the Western world.

The three sisters were constantly in the public eye and were treated like celebrities. They were fashionistas and dressed to fit their social status.

The sisters' husbands' politics eventually drove a wedge between the three women, as they held totally opposing political views. But in 1937, Japan invaded China, which inevitably brought the sisters back together. As part of the war effort, they helped run field hospitals and welfare projects. They also appealed to the West to help China during the Japanese invasion. In doing so, the sisters were influential in shaping China's relationship with the West.

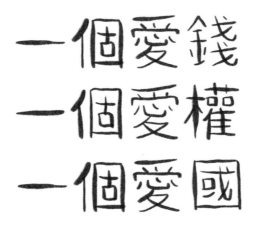

一個愛錢
一個愛權
一個愛國

The Seven Sutherland Sisters

American circus performers

Sarah (1846–1919), Victoria (1849–1902),
Isabella (1852–1914), Grace (1854–1946), Naomi (1858–1893),
Dora (1861–1926), Mary (1864–1939)

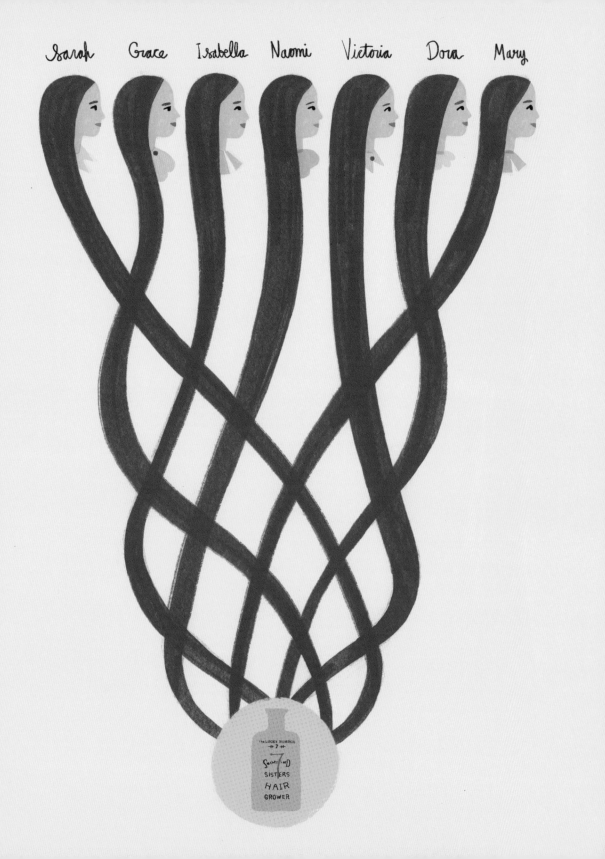

Sarah, Victoria, Isabella, Grace, Naomi, Dora, and Mary Sutherland had very long hair. So long that all together it was measured at thirty-seven feet! These seven sisters were singers and performers, and they played instruments onstage. But what the audience really came to see was their shockingly long hair. It was the Victorian era, and long flowing hair was the epitome of femininity. That being said, respectable women were expected to keep their hair up; letting hair loose was considered quite provocative. The sisters' audiences were mesmerized and enchanted by their flowing locks. So much so that the sisters' father created a tonic, which he claimed would grow such hair. He sold it at their performances, and the family quickly made millions, at a time when most Americans were struggling to earn a living. The sisters became huge celebrities and were featured in newspapers everywhere. They became a household name.

But they weren't always so glamorous.

The Sutherland sisters grew up on a turkey farm in Upstate New York. Their mother would rub smelly oil on their hair, since she believed it would make it grow strong and thick. But the smell drove away other children and left the sisters quite embarrassed. Their mother died when the youngest sister, Mary, was just a toddler. Their father, who wanted to make money beyond his farm income, started taking the girls to churches, fairs, and theaters to perform their singing. They gained a reputation for their voices . . . and for their hair, of course.

And that's how they began their glorious career. In 1880, the sisters made it to Broadway as the "the Seven Wonders." They toured all over the United States, and wherever they went, audiences stared in awe at their beautiful tresses, which at the time seemed magical, or even divine. They were so successful that by 1884 they joined Barnum and Bailey's Greatest Show on Earth as an attraction.

P. T. Barnum himself called them "the seven most pleasing wonders of the world." Naomi Sutherland, the fifth sister, even married J. Henry Bailey, nephew of James Anthony Bailey, co-owner of the circus. The seven sisters were clever businesswomen and came up with slogans to sell themselves as well as their father's ointment. For example, one of their slogans was "Ladies should always remember it's the hair—not the hat—that makes a woman attractive." They became outlandishly rich and lived an ostentatious and wild life, which got people speculating on whether they were practicing witchcraft. With time, their popularity declined. The sisters' final downfall came in 1920s, when flappers started to cut their hair short. (The flappers were women who broke with traditional gender norms by wearing loose clothing and cropped hair and by hanging out in public more than ever before.) Long hair was no longer in fashion, and the sisters faded into a distant memory.

Trưng Trac & Trưng Nhi

Vietnamese military leaders

Trac (circa 12–43 CE)
Nhi (circa 14–43 CE)

Sisters Trưng Trac and Trưng Nhi grew up in a noble family in rural Northern Vietnam. They were raised to be perfect noblewomen. At that time, it meant the sisters were trained to be excellent in both literature and martial arts! They were groomed to marry noblemen, as well as inherit their father's estate. Life was going according to plan, when something pretty dramatic happened. But let's back up a bit: the year was 40 CE, and the Chinese Han dynasty had ruled Vietnam for more than one hundred years. But the Vietnamese people wanted their independence, and one Vietnamese lord, Thi Sach of Chau Dien, decided to do something about it. This lord happened to be Trưng Trac's husband! He was accused of plotting against the Chinese and was executed by the cruel Chinese governor.

Trưng Trac was enraged, and she was not going to stay silent. She was a charismatic leader in her own right, and asked her fearless younger sister, Trưng Nhi, to join her mission to complete what her husband began—attaining freedom for Vietnam. The two of them called all the tribal chiefs to plan their attack on the Chinese.

According to legend, the sisters needed to prove themselves to the chiefs before getting their cooperation. So they performed acts of bravery, like killing a terrorizing tiger and using its skin as paper to write up their fiery proclamation. Once they

proved their leadership, the sisters gathered an
army of more than eighty thousand people. Many of
the fighters were women, including their own mother!
The sisters headed the very first Vietnamese rebellion
against the Chinese while riding on the backs of elephants.
They were pretty successful, and they caused the Chinese to
flee from sixty-five fortresses! Finally, they were able to form
an independant Vietnamese state. Trưng Trac became queen,
and Trưng Nhi her head adviser (though some say co-regent).

Sadly, their victory was short-lived, lasting only three years.
The massive Chinese military, under the leadership of emperor Ma Yuan,
came after them, and they were forced to retreat. The Trưng sisters were
devastated and could not face the terrible defeat. According to Vietnamese
tradition, they decided to die by suicide rather than be captured, and they
drowned themselves in the river in the year 43 BCE. (The Chinese version
of this story claims they were beheaded by Ma Yuan himself.)

To this day, the people of Vietnam are proud to have the Trưng sisters as
part of their national history. They have songs, stories, and plays dedicated
to these powerful female leaders. Every year, there are ceremonies for the
sisters at the Hai Bà ("Two Ladies") temple, located in Hanoi, the capital city
of Vietnam.

"Bloody" Mary
& Elizabeth I Tudor

English queens

Mary (1516–1558)
Elizabeth (1533–1603)

Poor Elizabeth. When she was only three years old, her mother, queen Anne Boleyn, was executed by her father, King Henry VIII. This left little Elizabeth with only her nanny, Kat Ashley, to count on. From a very young age, Elizabeth was quite serious and enjoyed solitary activities. One of her favorite pastimes was writing, anything from poems and prayers to powerful speeches.

Elizabeth had a half sister, Mary, who was seventeen years older. Mary was the daughter of Catherine of Aragon, King Henry's first wife. They were not close for many reasons. First, Mary hated Elizabeth's mother, Anne, for taking her own mother's place as queen. Also, Mary was a devout Catholic like her mother, while Elizabeth was a Protestant, like her father.

In 1553, Mary became queen. When she was crowned, she rode majestically into London. Elizabeth rode by Mary's side, but their supportive relationship did not last long. Mary was deeply religious; she wanted to make England Catholic again (after many years that it wasn't). She did not trust Elizabeth because she had different religious beliefs. Elizabeth's life was now in danger: Mary put her own sister in the Tower of London (a castle that was used as a prison) so Elizabeth could not lead a Protestant rebellion against her. Elizabeth just narrowly avoided the same fate as her own mother, but not so for others: Mary executed hundreds of Protestants, which gave her the nickname

"Bloody Mary." She became even more hated when in 1554 she married the king of Spain, Philip II, who was Catholic. Mary did not invite Elizabeth to her wedding. No surprise there!

But alas, Mary had no children, so when she died from an illness in 1558, her sister, Elizabeth, was the next in line to the throne. Elizabeth became queen and immediately made England Protestant again, to the whole kingdom's delight.

Next, it was expected that the queen get married and have children, but Elizabeth never did. It was said that she was married to her kingdom instead.

Even though she had a rough childhood, Elizabeth grew up to become a dearly beloved ruler (most of the time), and many called her "Good Queen Bess." She still loved writing and giving powerful speeches. She reigned for forty-five years in what was called the Elizabethan era, a golden age for England, full of prosperity and cultural riches. (For example, Shakespeare wrote all of his plays during her lifetime!)

Venus & Serena Williams

Professional American tennis players

Venus (born 1980)
Serena (born 1981)

Tennis players, world champions, legendary athletes, rivals.

And also sisters.

The Williams sisters' story is a rags-to-riches American fairy tale. Venus and Serena were both trained from a young age to play tennis by their father, Richard Williams, who taught himself to play from books and videos. The sisters grew up in a poor neighborhood in Compton, Southern California, and often trained in conditions that were not optimal to say the least; sometimes the tennis courts were strewn with broken glass and had no nets. But Richard had big dreams for his daughters, and his dream became theirs. The sisters were determined to become sports stars, the best players in the world.

Venus and Serena trained for several hours every day for years. When they were ten and twelve, the family moved to Florida so they could get professional coaching. The sisters improved with time, and when they were teenagers, they began to compete professionally. And they won medals in local tournaments!

But that was just the beginning. In 1999, at age seventeen, Serena won her first US Open, and Venus won a year later, in 2000. Both Venus and Serena have gone on to win multiple gold medals in the Olympics, were each ranked No. 1 in the world, and won many championships. Today, they are considered two of the best players in tennis history. The sisters became iconic, and they are recognized in popular culture by their first names alone. They are adored worldwide for their strength and excellence. Though in many tennis matches they compete against each other, the sisters remain close. Sometimes they even play side by side: the pair won several gold medals in women's doubles at the Olympics.

Throughout their amazing careers, the sisters experienced bumps along the way. They both incurred various injuries and had to face racism and racial bias. Despite these setbacks, the sisters persevered. Serena took a break from the game to have her daughter in 2017 but returned to compete after her pregnancy and its subsequent complications. It has been a long road, but the sisters achieved their dreams of becoming two of the best tennis players in the world.

Virginia Woolf & Vanessa Bell

English author and painter

Vanessa (1879–1961)
Virginia (1882–1941)

Vanessa

Virginia

When Vanessa and her younger sister Virginia were children, they made a pact: Vanessa would be the painter, and Virginia would be the writer. The sisters were surrounded by art from birth. Their father was a London-based editor and literary critic, and their mother was a beautiful socialite with lots of artistic connections, so the sisters lived in an environment that encouraged their creative tendencies.

The two sisters were quite competitive and often jealous of each other, but even with these feelings, they remained close throughout their lives and relied on one other for comfort and support. They had many nicknames for one another; for example, Virginia was "Billy" and Vanessa was "Dolphin." Their mother died when the girls were young teenagers, so in many ways Vanessa took on a maternal role with regard to her sister. She was very supportive of Virginia, who suffered from anxiety and depression.

The sisters grew up to fulfill their childhood dreams: Virginia became a groundbreaking and world-famous writer, with classics such as the novel *Mrs. Dalloway* and the feminist essay "A Room of One's Own." Vanessa, who is lesser known (and somewhat overshadowed by Virginia), became a painter and a designer, and she exhibited her work in several galleries in London. Vanessa and Virginia collaborated artistically with one another:

Vanessa designed book covers for all of Virginia's books and even illustrated one of Virginia's short stories. Virginia in turn sat as a model while Vanessa painted. She also based several of her novel characters on Vanessa (some say *To the Lighthouse* is based on her).

Vanessa's and Virginia's lives were far from boring. Together, the sisters belonged to the "Bloomsbury Group," a bohemian and radical circle of artists and thinkers in London who led free-spirited and untraditional lifestyles.

Sadly, Virginia continued to suffer from depression throughout her life, and at the age of fifty-nine she drowned herself in the River Ouse in Northern Yorkshire. To this day, Virginia is an inspiration to many, and she is commemorated in films, fine art, literature, and plays.

Suggested Further Reading

- Adams, Julia. 2018. *101 Awesome Women Who Changed Our World*. Arcturus Publishing Limited.

- Alvarez, Julia. 2010. *In the Time of the Butterflies*. Algonquin Books.

- Conkling, Winifred. 2015. *Passenger on the Pearl: The True Story of Emily Edmonson's Flight from Slavery*. Algonquin Young Readers.

- Eding, June. 2008. *Who Was Queen Elizabeth?*. Penguin Young Readers Group.

- Gilpin, Caroline. 2013. *National Geographic Readers: Amelia Earhart*. National Geographic Children's Books.

- Henry, Joanne Landers. 1996. *Elizabeth Blackwell: Girl Doctor*. Aladdin.

- Herman, Gail. 2017. *Who Was Coretta Scott King?*. Penguin Young Readers Group.

- Hooks, Gwendolyn. 2017. *If You Were a Kid During the Civil Rights Movement*. Scholastic, Inc.

- McNamara, Margaret. 2018. *Eliza: The Story of Elizabeth Schuyler Hamilton*. Random House Children's Books.

- Rau, Dana Meachen. 2015. *Who Was Harriet Beecher Stowe?*. Penguin Young Readers Group.

Sources

Introduction

Tannen, Deborah. "Why Sisterly Chats Make People Happier." *New York Times*, October 25, 2010. https://www.nytimes.com/2010/10/26/health/26essay.html.

"20 Things You'll Only Understand If You Have a Sister." *Good Housekeeping*, March 27, 2019. https://www.goodhousekeeping.com/life/a45376/things-you-will-understand-if-you-are-sisters/.

Alcott Sisters

"Abba May Alcott Nieriker." Louisa May Alcott's Orchard House. Accessed September 26, 2020. https://louisamayalcott.org/abba-may-alcott-nieriker.

Alcott, Louisa May, and May Alcott. 2008. *Little Women Abroad: The Alcott Sisters' Letters from Europe, 1870–1871*. University of Georgia Press.

Appleby, Joyce, Eileen Chang, and Neva Goodwin. 2002. *Encyclopedia of Women in American History*. Routledge.

Andrews Sisters

"The Andrews Sisters." Encyclopedia Britannica, June 26, 2019. https://www.britannica.com/topic/the-Andrews-Sisters.

Blaszyk, Amy. "Patty Andrews, Leader of the Andrews Sisters, Dies." NPR, January 30, 2013. https://www.npr.org/sections/therecord/2013/01/31/133568889/patty-andrews-leader-of-the-andrews-sisters-dies.

Sforza, John. *Swing It!: The Andrews Sisters Story*. University Press of Kentucky.

Azmi Sisters

Ormsby, Mary. "Five Toronto Sisters Challenge Stereotypes to Carry on Ball Hockey Tradition." *Star*, August 11, 2017. https://www.thestar.com/news/gta/2017/08/11/five-toronto-sisters-challenge-stereotypes-to-carry-on-ball-hockey-tradition.html.

Rush, Curtis. "The Azmi Sisters Go Hard in Ball Hockey. Don't Act So Surprised." *New York Times*, July 29, 2018. https://www.nytimes.com/2018/07/29/sports/azmi-sisters-ball-hockey.html.

Balbusso Sisters

"Anna + Elena = Balbusso Twins Illustrations." Accessed September 26, 2020. http://www.balbusso.com/.

Heller, Steven. "Two Twins, One Design Career." *Atlantic*, July 17, 2013. https://www.theatlantic.com/entertainment/archive/2012/03/two-twins-one-design-career/255202/.

Smetts, Bonnie. "Anna+Elena Balbusso." Communication Arts, October 6, 2010. https://www.commarts.com/features/anna-elena-balbusso.

Beecher Sisters

Beecher, Catharine, and Harriet Beecher Stowe. 1869. *American Woman's Home: Or, Principles of Domestic Science*. J. B. Ford & Company.

Sklar, Kathryn Kish. 1976. *Catharine Beecher: A Study in American Domesticity*. Norton.

Vollaro, Daniel R. 2009. "Lincoln, Stowe, and the 'Little Woman/Great War' Story: The Making, and Breaking, of a Great American Anecdote." *Journal of the Abraham Lincoln Association*, 30 (1). Michigan Publishing, University of Michigan Library. Accessed September 26, 2020.

https://quod.lib.umich.edu/j/jala/2629860.0030.104/--lincoln-stowe-and
-the-little-womangreat-war-story-the-making?rgn=main;view=fulltext.

Blackwell Sisters

Kline, Nancy. 1997. *Elizabeth Blackwell: A Doctor's Triumph, First Woman M.D.* Conari Press.

"Women of the Blackwell Family." Radcliffe Institute for Advanced Study at Harvard University, August 23, 2016. https://www.radcliffe.harvard .edu/schlesinger-library/exhibition/women-blackwell-family.

Bouvier Sisters

Kashner, Sam, and Nancy Schoenberger. 2018. *The Fabulous Bouvier Sisters: The Tragic and Glamorous Lives of Jackie and Lee.* HarperCollins.

"Life of Jacqueline B. Kennedy." John F. Kennedy Presidential Library and Museum. Accessed September 26, 2020. https://www.jfklibrary.org/ learn/about-jfk/life-of-jacqueline-b-kennedy.

Taraborrelli, J. Randy. 2018. *Jackie, Janet & Lee: The Secret Lives of Janet Auchincloss and Her Daughters Jacqueline Kennedy Onassis and Lee Radziwill.* St. Martin's Press.

Brontë Sisters

Ackroyd, Peter. "The Sublimely Inaccurate Portrait of the Brontë Sisters." *New Yorker*, September 11, 1995. https://www.newyorker.com/ magazine/1995/09/18/the-three-sisters.

Harman, Claire. 2016. *Charlotte Brontë: A Fiery Heart.* Knopf Canada.

Lutz, Deborah. 2015. *The Brontë Cabinet: Three Lives in Nine Objects.* W. W. Norton & Company.

Cone Sisters

Feinberg, Harriet. "Etta Cone." Jewish Women's Archive. Accessed September 26, 2020. https://jwa.org/encyclopedia/article/cone-etta.

Hirschland, Ellen B., and Nancy Hirschland Ramage. 2008. *The Cone Sisters of Baltimore: Collecting at Full Tilt*. Northwestern University Press.

Malino, Sarah S. "Claribel Cone." Jewish Women's Archive. Accessed September 26, 2020. https://jwa.org/encyclopedia/article/cone-claribel.

Winkler, Joseph. "Sister Act." *Tablet*, June 10, 2011. https://www.tabletmag.com/sections/arts-letters/articles/sister-act-2.

Cook Sisters

Cook, Ida. 2008. *Safe Passage: The Remarkable True Story of Two Sisters Who Rescued Jews from the Nazis*. Harlequin.

Smith, Lyn. 2012. *Heroes of the Holocaust: Ordinary Britons Who Risked Their Lives to Make a Difference*. Ebury Press.

"Spy Mystery of British Sisters Who Helped Jewish Refugees Flee the Nazis." *Guardian*, November 5, 2017. https://www.theguardian.com/world/2017/nov/05/ida-louise-cook-sisters-helped-jewish-refugees-flee-nazis-spy-mystery-film.

"The Opera-Loving Sisters Who 'Stumbled' into Heroism." BBC, January 28, 2017. https://www.bbc.com/news/uk-england-tyne-38732779.

Dann Sisters

American Outrage. 2008. Directed by Beth Gage and George Gage. First Run Features.

"International Day for the Elimination of Violence against Women." United Nations. Accessed September 26, 2020. https://www.un.org/womenwatch/daw/news/vawd.html.

"Mary and Carrie Dann of the Western Shoshone Nation." Right
Livelihood Foundation. Accessed September 26, 2020. https://
www.rightlivelihoodaward.org/laureates/mary-and-carrie-dann-of
-the-western-shoshone-nation/.

Mitchell, Saundra. 2016. *50 Unbelievable Women and Their Fascinating
(and True!) Stories (They Did What?)*. Puffin Books.

Delany Sisters

Hearth, Amy Hill, Annie Elizabeth Delany, and Sarah Louise Delany. 1993.
Having Our Say: The Delany Sisters' First 100 Years. Kodansha America.

Severo, Richard. "Sadie Delany, Witness to Century, Dies at 109." *New York
Times*, January 26, 1999. https://www.nytimes.com/1999/01/26/
nyregion/sadie-delany-witness-to-century-dies-at-109.html.

Earhart Sisters

Fleming, Candace. 2011. *Amelia Lost: The Life and Disappearance of
Amelia Earhart*. Schwartz & Wade.

"Grace Muriel Earhart Morrissey." Ninety-Nines, Inc. Accessed September
26, 2020. https://www.ninety-nines.org/grace-muriel-earhart-morrissey.html.

Rich, Doris L. 2013. *Amelia Earhart: A Biography*. Smithsonian.

Edmonson Sisters

"The Edmonson Sisters Life Story." Women and the American Story
curriculum guide. New York Historical Society. 2017. https://
www.nyhistory.org/womens-history/education/curriculum/saving
-washington/module-2-breaking-the-rules-women/life-stories/emily
-and-mary-edmonson.

"Escape from Slavery: The Story of Mary and Emily Edmonson."

Footnoting History, September 8, 2018. https://www.footnotinghistory
.com/home/escape-from-slavery-the-story-of-mary-and-emily-edmonson.

Harper, C. W. 1985. "Black Aristocrats: Domestic Servants on the
Antebellum Plantation." *Phylon* 46 (2): 123–35.

Gabor Sisters

Handy, Bruce. "Glamour and Goulash." *Vanity Fair*, October 4, 2010.
https://www.vanityfair.com/news/2001/07/zsa-zsa-200107.

McFadden, Robert D. "Zsa Zsa Gabor, Actress Famous for Her Glamour
(and Her Marriages), Dies at 99." *New York Times*, December 18, 2016.
https://www.nytimes.com/2016/12/18/movies/zsa-zsa-gabor-often
-married-actress-known-for-glamour-dies.html.

Porter, Darwin. 2013. *Those Glamorous Gabors: Bombshells from Budapest*.
Blood Moon Productions.

Turtu, Anthony, and Donald F. Reuter. 2001. *Gaborabilia: An Illustrated
Celebration of the Fabulous, Legendary Gabor Sisters*. Three Rivers Press.

Grimké Sisters

"About the Grimke Sisters." Louise W. Knight. Accessed September 26,
2020. https://www.louisewknight.com/about-the-grimke-sisters.html.

Appleby, Joyce, Eileen Chang, and Neva Goodwin. 2002. *Encyclopedia of
Women in American History*. Routledge.

Knight, Louise. "Louise Knight: How Massachusetts Women Became
Political." Radcliffe Institute for Advanced Study at Harvard University,
July 20, 2015. https://www.radcliffe.harvard.edu/video/louise
-knight-how-massachusetts-women-became-political.

Perry, Mark. 2001. *Lift Up Thy Voice: The Sarah and Angelina Grimké
Family's Journey from Slaveholders to Civil Rights Leaders*. Viking.

Harris Sisters

Goodyear, Dana, Benjamin Wallace-Wells, and Eren Orbey. "Kamala Harris Makes Her Case." *New Yorker*, July 22, 2019. https://www .newyorker.com/magazine/2019/07/22/kamala-harris-makes-her-case.

Harris, Kamala. 2019. *This Truths We Hold: An American Journey.* Penguin Books.

Igoe, Katherine J. "Who Is Maya Harris, Kamala Harris; Super-Supportive Sister?" *Marie Claire*, August 12, 2020. https://www.marieclaire.com/ politics/amp33584035/who-is-maya-harris-kamala-harris-sister/.

Terris, Ben. "Who Is the Real Kamala Harris? Her Sister, Maya, Knows the Answer." *Washington Post*, July 23, 2019. https://www.washingtonpost .com/lifestyle/2019/07/23/who-is-real-kamala-harris-her-sister-maya -knows-answer/?arc404=true.

Hyers Sisters

Buckner, Jocelyn L. 2012. "Spectacular Opacities": The Hyers Sisters' Performances of Respectability and Resistance." *African American Review* 45 (3): 309–23.

Hine, Darlene Clark, and Kathleen Thompson. 1998. *A Shining Thread of Hope: The History of Black Women in America.* Broadway Books.

Malone, Jacqui. 1996. *Steppin' on the Blues: The Visible Rhythms of African American Dance.* University of Illinois Press.

Norah Jones and Anoushka Shankar

"Anoushka Shankar Biography." Accessed September 26, 2020. https:// www.anoushkashankar.com/biography/.

"Coming to India Is Bittersweet: Norah Jones." *Hindustan Times*, February 23, 2013. https://www.hindustantimes.com/brunch/coming-to-india

-is-bittersweet-norah-jones/story-66GH8TS80wEgTBwzRMiKEM.html.

Erlewine, Stephen Thomas. "Norah Jones: Biography & History." AllMusic. Accessed September 26, 2020. https://www.allmusic.com/artist/norah -jones-mn0000884686/biography.

"Norah Jones." Bluenote.com. Accessed September 26, 2020. http://www .bluenote.com/artist/norah-jones/.

Steve Cummins. "Anoushka Shankar's Life Story Is Stranger than Fiction." *Irish Examiner*, June 23, 2016. https://www.irishexaminer.com/lifestyle/ arid-20406388.html.

Kardashian/Jenner Sisters

Bliss, Sara. "Kim Kardashian Is Becoming a Lawyer: What Her Move Can Teach You About Making a Career Leap." *Forbes Magazine*, April 21, 2019. https://www.forbes.com/sites/sarabliss/2019/04/18/kim -kardashian-is-becoming-a-lawyer-what-her-move-can-teach-you -about-making-a-career-leap/.

"Forbes Billionaires 2020." *Forbes Magazine*. Accessed September 26, 2020. https://www.forbes.com/billionaires/.

Smith, Josh. "The Kardashian Family Tree: Who's Who in America's Most Famous Family." *Glamour UK*, September 9, 2020. https://www .glamourmagazine.co.uk/gallery/kardashian-family-tree.

Knowles Sisters

"Beyoncé." Encyclopedia Britannica, August 31, 2020. https://www .britannica.com/biography/Beyonce.

Knowles-Carter, Beyoncé. "Beyoncé in Her Own Words: Her Life, Her Body, Her Heritage." *Vogue*, August 6, 2018. https://www.vogue.com/

article/beyonce-september-issue-2018.

Mathis, Ayana. "Solange, the Polymathic Cultural Force." *New York Times*, October 15, 2018. https://www.nytimes.com/2018/10/15/t-magazine/ solange-interview.html.

Taraborrelli, J. Randy. 2015. *Becoming Beyoncé: The Untold Story*. Grand Central Publishing.

Ann Landers and Abigail Van-Buren

"Birth of Advice-Givers Ann Landers and Abigail Van Buren." Jewish Women's Archive, July 4, 1918. https://jwa.org/thisweek/jul/04/1918/ ann-landers-and-abigail-van-buren.

Kogan, Rick. 2003. *America's Mom: The Life, Lessons, and Legacy of Ann Landers*. William Morrow.

Shapiro, Samantha M. "Who Was Dear Abby?" *New York Times*, December 22, 2013. https://www.nytimes.com/news/the-lives-they -lived/2013/12/21/abigail-van-buren/.

Van Buren, Abigail. 1981. *The Best of Dear Abby*. Andrews and McMeel.

MacDonald Sisters

Green, Cynthia. "The Scottish Sisters Who Pioneered Art Nouveau." Daily Jstor, December 19, 2017. https://daily.jstor.org/the-scottish-sisters-who -pioneered-art-nouveau/.

Helland, Janice. 1993. "Frances Macdonald: The Self as Fin-De-Siècle Woman." *Woman's Art Journal* 14 (1): 15–22.

Jones, Claire E. 2011. "The Macdonald Sisters: How They Visually Created Equality Between Men and Women." *Inquiries Journal/Student Pulse*, 3(09). http://www.inquiriesjournal.com/articles/573/the-macdonald

-sisters-how-they-visually-created-equality-between-men-and-women.

Weltge, Sigrid W. 1987. "Women in Design: Will They Find Their Place in History?" *Women's Studies Quarterly* 15 (1/2): 58–61.

Malik Sisters

"Malik Twins Complete Explorers Grand Slam." *India Today*, July 9, 2015. https://www.indiatoday.in/india/video/grand-slam-tashi-nancy-malik -twins-youngest-mount-everest-431824-2015-07-08.

"Tashi and Nungshi Malik, Passionate Mountaineers and Guinness World Record Holders." Armadillo. Accessed September 26, 2020. https:// armadillomerino.com/blogs/champions/005-tashi-and-nungshi -malik-passionate-mountaineers-and-guinness-world-record-holders.

Manziaris Sisters

"2017 Gabby Awards Honorees Linda & Susanna Manziaris." Greek America Foundation YouTube Channel, June 24, 2017. https://www .youtube.com/watch?v=EEfjrBAqZv8.

"Girls Helping Girls! Linda and Susanna Manziaris." *Breakfast Television Toronto*, December 24, 2013. https://www.bttoronto.ca/ videos/2968255151001/.

Kokshanian, Rita. "Shop for a Cause: Meet the 14-Year-Old Jewelry Designer Who's Funding Women's Education." *InStyle*, July 12, 2014. https://www.instyle.com/news/shop-cause-meet-14-year-old-jewelry -designer-whos-funding-womens-education.

Pappas, Gregory. "Two Teen-Aged Canadian Sisters Changing the World: Meet Susanna and Linda Manziaris." *Pappas Post*, October 22, 2015. https://www.pappaspost.com/two-teen-aged-canadian-sisters-changing -the-world-meet-susanna-and-linda-manziaris/.

White, Shelley. "Generation Z: The Kids Who'll Save the World?" *Globe and Mail*, September 25, 2014. https://www.theglobeandmail.com/life/giving/generation-z-the-kids-wholl-save-the-world/article20790237/.

McFadden Sisters

"About Tatyana." Tatyana McFadden. Accessed September 26, 2020. https://www.tatyanamcfadden.com/about-tatyana/.

"Hannah McFadden." Team USA. Accessed September 26, 2020. https://www.teamusa.org/para-track-and-field/athletes/Hannah-McFadden.

Klingaman, Mike. "Inseparable McFadden Sisters Bond over Sports, Will Compete in Paralympics Track and Field." *Baltimore Sun*, September 7, 2016. https://www.baltimoresun.com/sports/olympics/bs-sp-paralympics-mcfaddens-xxxx-20160907-story.html.

"Tatyana McFadden." Team USA. Accessed September 26, 2020. https://www.teamusa.org/para-track-and-field/athletes/Tatyana-McFadden.

Whiteside, Kelly. "A Paralympian Races to Remove Obstacles for the Next Generation." *New York Times*, September 1, 2016. https://www.nytimes.com/2016/09/04/sports/olympics/paralympics-tatyana-mcfadden-wheelchair.html.

Middleton Sisters

Andersen, Christopher. 2011. *William and Kate: A Royal Love Story*. Simon and Schuster.

Joseph, Claudia. 2010. *Kate: Kate Middleton Princess in Waiting*. Mainstream Publishing Company, Limited.

Nicholl, Katie. 2015. *Kate: The Future Queen*. Hachette Books.

"Pippa Middleton Named *Vanity Fair* Contributing Editor, Writes About Her (and Kate's) Tennis Obsession." *Vanity Fair*, June 5, 2013. https://www.vanityfair.com/news/2013/06/pippa-middleton-columnist-tennis.

Mirabal Sisters

Jewell, Hannah. 2018. *She Caused a Riot, 100 Unknown Women Who Built Cities, Sparked Revolutions, & Massively Crushed It*. Sourcebooks.

Lee, Mackenzi. 2018. *Bygone Badass Broads, 52 Forgotten Women Who Changed the World*. Audible Studios.

Mulleavy Sisters

Fortini, Amanda, Kelefa Sanneh, and Rebecca Mead. "The Sisters Behind Rodarte." *New Yorker*, January 18, 2010. https://www.newyorker.com/magazine/2010/01/18/twisted-sisters.

"The Official Website of Rodarte." Accessed September 26, 2020. http://www.rodarte.net/.

Peretz, Evgenia. "The Rodarte Effect." *Vanity Fair*, February 9, 2012. https://www.vanityfair.com/style/2012/03/rodarte-201203.

Valenti, Lauren, Steff Yotka, Janelle Okwodu, Brooke Bobb, and Rachel Hahn. "Rodarte News, Collections, Fashion Shows, Fashion Week Reviews, and More." *Vogue*. Accessed September 26, 2020. https://www.vogue.com/fashion-shows/designer/rodarte.

Whitney, Christine. "The Sisters Behind Rodarte on Sharing Everything Except Clothes." *The Cut*, February 5, 2018. https://www.thecut.com/2018/02/the-sisters-behind-rodarte-share-everything-except-clothes.html.

Obama Sisters

Jean-Philippe, McKenzie. "Malia and Sasha Obama Give Their First Public Interview in Netflix's 'Becoming.'" *O, Oprah Magazine*, May 5, 2020. https://www.oprahmag.com/entertainment/books/a32362642/malia-and-sasha-obama-netflix-becoming/.

Obama, Michelle. 2018. *Becoming*. Crown Publishing.

Robertson, Hamish. "The Obama Code Names Explained." *Vanity Fair*, November 13, 2008. https://www.vanityfair.com/news/2008/11/the -obama-code-names-explained/amp.

Olsen Sisters

Alexander, Ella. "Elizabeth Olsen: Inside the Surprisingly Low-Key World of a Marvel Superhero." *Harper's Bazaar*, April 17, 2018. https://www .harpersbazaar.com/uk/culture/a19840824/elizabeth-olsen -interview-avengers/.

Binkley, Christina. "Mary-Kate and Ashley Olsen's The Row Launches Menswear." *Wall Street Journal Magazine*, August 27, 2018. https://www .wsj.com/articles/mary-kate-and-ashley-olsens-the-row-launches -menswear-1535371228.

Marine, Brooke. "Mary-Kate and Ashley Olsen Would Like to Remind You That They Are Still Two Separate People." *W Magazine*, August 27, 2018. https://www.wmagazine.com/story/mary-kate-ashley-olsen-differences -the-row-mens/amp/.

Peters Sisters

Corbett, Merlisa Lawrence. "Remembering the First Pair of African-American Sisters to Take Tennis by Storm." Bleacher Report, October 2, 2017. https://bleacherreport.com/articles/2353528-remembering-the -first-pair-of-african-american-sisters-to-take-tennis-by-storm.

Estrada, Louie. "Tennis Champion Matilda Walker Dies at 85." *Washington Post*, May 21, 2003. https://www.washingtonpost.com/archive/local/ 2003/05/21/tennis-champion-matilda-walker-dies-at-85/6b964699-9a19

-4421-9baf-d2e17153f866/?noredirect=on&utm_term=.a731335bd0df.

Fitzgerald, Natalie. "Margaret (1915–2004) and Matilda (1917–2003) Peters." Blackpast, July 8, 2018. https://www.blackpast.org/african-american -history/peters-margaret-1915-2004-and-matilda-1917-2003/.

Podgórska Sisters

Atwood, Kathryn J. 2011. *Women Heroes of World War II: 26 Stories of Espionage, Sabotage, Resistance, and Rescue.* Chicago Review Press.

Kennedy, J. Michael. 1995. "Sisters Reunited with Jews They Saved from Nazis: World War II: Unlikely Protectors Were Youngsters When They Hid 13 People in a Cramped Polish Apartment." *Los Angeles Times*, January 10, 1995. https://www.latimes.com/archives/la-xpm-1995-01 -10-mn-18462-story.html.

"Oral History Interview with Stefania Podgórska Burzminski." Interviewed by Linda G. Kuzmack, the Unites States Holocaust Memorial Museum. September 22, 1989. https://collections.ushmm.org/search/catalog/ irn504548.

"The Righteous Among the Nations Database." Yad Vashem. Accessed September 26, 2020. https://righteous.yadvashem.org/index .html?language=en.

Ross Sisters

"Beyond Skin Deep: Promoting Diversity in Medical School." American Association of Colleges of Osteopathic Medicine. Accessed September 26, 2020. https://www.aacom.org/become-a-doctor/diversity-in-ome/ barbara-ross-lee.

Ross, Diana. 1993. *Secrets of a Sparrow.* Villard Books.

Taraborrelli, J. Randy. 2007. *Diana Ross: A Biography.* Citadel Press.

Schuyler Sisters

Davies, Monika. 2017. *The Schuyler Sisters*. Teacher Created Materials.

"The Schuyler Sisters and Their Circle". Albany Institute of History and Art, July 20–December 29, 2019. https://www.albanyinstitute.org/the-schuyler-sisters-and-their-circle.html.

Scott Sisters

Bagley, Edythe Scott, and Bernice King. 2012. *Desert Rose: The Life and Legacy of Coretta Scott King*. University Alabama Press.

Medearis, Angela Shelf. 1999. *Dare to Dream: Coretta Scott King and the Civil Rights Movement*. Puffin Books.

Waxman, Laura Hamilton. 2008. *Coretta Scott King*. Lerner Publishing Group.

Soong Sisters

Donovan, Sandy. 2006. *Madame Chiang Kai-Shek: Face of Modern China*. Compass Point Books.

Hahn, Emily. 2003. *The Soong Sisters*. Open Road Media.

Li, Laura Tyson. 2006. *Madame Chiang Kai-Shek: China's Eternal First Lady*. Grove Press.

Peterson, Barbara Bennett. 2000. *Notable Women of China: Shang Dynasty to the Early 20th Century*. M. E. Sharpe Publishing.

Sutherland Sisters

Hix, Lisa. "Untangling the Tale of the Seven Sutherland Sisters and Their 37 Feet of Hair." Collectors Weekly, September 6, 2013. https://www.collectorsweekly.com/articles/the-seven-sutherland-sisters-and-their-37-feet-of-hair/.

Lewis, Clarence. 1991. *The Seven Sutherland Sisters*. Niagara County Historical Society.

Trưng Sisters

Salmonson, Jessica Amanda. 1991. *The Encyclopedia of Amazons: Women Warriors from Antiquity to the Modern Era*. Paragon House.

Vo, Nghia M, and Nguyen Ngoc Bich. 2015. *The Trung Sisters Revisited*. CreateSpace.

"Bloody" Mary and Elizabeth I Tudor

Borman, Tracy. 2016. *The Private Lives of the Tudors: Uncovering the Secrets of Britain's Greatest Dynasty*. Grove Press.

Marcus, Leah S., Janel Mueller, and Mary Beth Rose. 2000. *Elizabeth I: Collected Works*. University of Chicago Press.

Williams Sisters

Crawford, E. J. "Black History Month Legends: Venus and Serena." United States Tennis Association, February 27, 2017. https://www.usta.com/en/home/stay-current/national/black-history-month-legends--serena-and-venus-williams.html.

Pak, Eudie. "Serena Williams and 7 Female Tennis Players Who've Endured Controversy." Biography.com. May 28, 2020. https://www.biography.com/news/serena-williams-female-tennis-players-controversy-scandal.

Williams, Serena, Hilary Beard, and Venus Williams. 2005. *Venus and Serena: Serving from the Hip: 10 Rules for Living, Loving, and Winning*. HMH Books for Young Readers.

Virginia Woolf and Vanessa Bell

Dunn, Jane. 1990. *A Very Close Conspiracy: Vanessa Bell and Virginia Woolf.* Little Brown.

Harris, Alexandra. 2015. *Virginia Woolf.* Thames & Hudson.

Roiphe, Katie. 2007. *Uncommon Arrangements.* Random House.

Sasseen, Rhian. "Vanessa Bell, Virginia Woolf and the Power of Sisterhood." Art UK, May 30, 2018. https://artuk.org/discover/stories/vanessa-bell-virginia-woolf-and-the-power-of-sisterhood.

Acknowledgments

I'm incredibly lucky to have four siblings—two sisters and two brothers. Thank you to Deena, Amitai, Darya, and Boaz, and to my sister-in-law, Michal, for sharing so many beautiful memories and for their friendship.

Thank you to my husband, Yitz, for being a constant source of encouragement and cheerleading.

Thank you to my daughters, Nevae, Kayla, and Romie, for being wonderful sisters to each other and for their biggest hearts.

Thanks to my dear grandma Esther for sharing fond memories of her sister Etta.

Thank you to my parents, Susan and Yedidya, for all their support and love.

I'm incredibly thankful to the amazing women who helped me with this book and who believed in it from the start: to my patient and insightful editor, Karen Chaplin, and to my agent, Anne Moore Armstrong, for making everything happen.

Finally, to all the sisters in this book, from whom I learned so much—thank you for being strong women and inspirational sisters.